Cupcakes

Sensational Sweet Treats for Any Occasion

Publications International, Ltd.

Pictured on the front cover: Strawberry Milkshake Cupcakes *(page 86)*.
Pictured on the back cover: Easter Chicks *(page 150)* and Pistachio-Chocolate Chip Cupcakes *(page 76)*.

ISBN-13: 978-1-4508-5289-0
ISBN-10: 1-4508-5289-0

Library of Congress Control Number: 2012934463

Manufactured in China.

8 7 6 5 4 3 2 1

Microwave Cooking: Microwave ovens vary in wattage. Use the cooking times as guidelines and check for doneness before adding more time.

Preparation/Cooking Times: Preparation times are based on the approximate amount of time required to assemble the recipe before cooking, baking, chilling or serving. These times include preparation steps such as measuring, chopping and mixing. The fact that some preparations and cooking can be done simultaneously is taken into account. Preparation of optional ingredients and serving suggestions is not included.

Publications International, Ltd.

Contents

Classic Cupcakes

Cream Cheese Cupcakes

        3 packages (8 ounces each) cream cheese, softened
        5 eggs
    1¼ cups sugar, divided
    2½ teaspoons vanilla, divided
        1 container (16 ounces) sour cream
        1 cup chopped fresh pitted cherries, fresh blueberries and canned
            crushed pineapple, drained

1. Preheat oven to 325°F. Line 24 standard (2½-inch) muffin cups with paper baking cups.

2. Beat cream cheese, eggs, 1 cup sugar and 1½ teaspoons vanilla in large bowl with electric mixer at medium speed 2 minutes or until well blended. Spoon evenly into prepared muffin cups.

3. Bake 20 minutes or until light golden brown. Cool in pans 5 minutes. (Centers of cupcakes will sink slightly.) Do not remove cupcakes from pans.

4. Combine sour cream, remaining ¼ cup sugar and 1 teaspoon vanilla in medium bowl; stir until blended. Fill depression in cupcakes with sour cream mixture. Bake 5 minutes. Cool in pans 10 minutes. Remove to wire racks; cool completely.

5. Top cupcakes with fruit topping.   *Makes 24 cupcakes*

Coconut Cupcakes

1 package DUNCAN HINES® Moist Deluxe® Butter Recipe Golden Cake Mix
3 eggs
1 cup (8 ounces) dairy sour cream
⅔ cup cream of coconut
¼ cup (½ stick) butter or margarine, softened
2 containers (16 ounces each) DUNCAN HINES® Creamy Home-Style Coconut Supreme Frosting

1. Preheat oven to 375°F. Place paper liners into 36 standard (2½-inch) muffin cups.

2. Combine cake mix, eggs, sour cream, cream of coconut and butter in large bowl. Beat at low speed with electric mixer until blended. Beat at medium speed 4 minutes. Fill paper liners half full. Bake at 375°F for 17 to 19 minutes or until toothpick inserted into centers comes out clean. Cool in pans 5 minutes. Remove to cooling racks. Cool completely. Frost cupcakes. Garnish with toasted coconut, if desired.

Makes 36 cupcakes

Tip: To toast coconut, spread evenly on baking sheet. Bake at 350°F for 3 minutes. Stir and bake 1 to 2 minutes longer or until golden brown.

Banana Chocolate-Chunk Cupcakes

2¼ cups all-purpose flour
2 teaspoons baking powder
1 teaspoon baking soda
½ teaspoon ground cinnamon
¼ teaspoon salt
1 cup sugar
½ cup (1 stick) butter, softened
2 eggs
3 ripe bananas, mashed
2 teaspoons vanilla
1 cup sour cream
5 squares (5 ounces) semisweet chocolate, cut into chunks
1¼ cups prepared chocolate frosting

1. Preheat oven to 350°F. Line 20 standard (2½-inch) muffin cups with paper baking cups.

2. Combine flour, baking powder, baking soda, cinnamon and salt in medium bowl; mix well. Beat sugar and butter in large bowl with electric mixer at medium speed until light and fluffy. Add eggs, one at a time, beating well after each addition. Add bananas and vanilla; beat until well blended. Alternately add flour mixture and sour cream, beating well after each addition. Stir in chocolate chunks. Spoon evenly into prepared muffin cups.

3. Bake 25 minutes or until toothpick inserted into centers comes out clean. Cool in pans 10 minutes. Remove to wire racks; cool completely.

4. Place frosting in pastry bag fitted with medium star tip; pipe rosettes on cupcakes.

Makes 20 cupcakes

Cookies & Cream Cupcakes

2¼ cups all-purpose flour
1⅔ cups sugar
  1 tablespoon baking powder
½ teaspoon salt
  1 cup milk
½ cup (1 stick) butter, softened
  2 teaspoons vanilla
  3 egg whites
  1 cup crushed chocolate sandwich cookies (about 10 cookies),
     plus additional for garnish
  1 container (16 ounces) vanilla frosting

1. Preheat oven to 350°F. Line 24 standard (2½-inch) muffin cups with paper baking cups.

2. Combine flour, sugar, baking powder and salt in large bowl; mix well. Add milk, butter and vanilla; beat with electric mixer at low speed 30 seconds. Beat at medium speed 2 minutes. Add egg whites; beat 2 minutes. Stir in 1 cup crushed cookies. Spoon evenly into prepared muffin cups.

3. Bake 20 minutes or until toothpick inserted into centers comes out clean. Cool in pans 10 minutes. Remove to wire racks; cool completely.

4. Frost cupcakes; sprinkle with additional crushed cookies.

Makes 24 cupcakes

Pineapple Coconut Cupcakes

1 package (about 18 ounces) white cake mix
1 can (12 ounces) lemon-lime soda
1 egg
1 egg white
2 tablespoons canola oil
1 can (20 ounces) crushed pineapple in its own juice
1 tablespoon plus 1 teaspoon cornstarch
2 cups whipped topping
½ cup flaked sweetened coconut, toasted*

*To toast coconut, spread evenly on ungreased baking sheet. Bake in preheated 350°F oven 5 to 7 minutes or until light golden brown, stirring occasionally.

1. Preheat oven to 350°F. Line 24 standard (2½-inch) muffin cups with paper baking cups.

2. Beat cake mix, soda, egg, egg white and oil in large bowl with electric mixer at low speed 30 seconds or until moistened. Beat at medium speed 2 minutes. Spoon evenly into prepared muffin cups.

3. Bake 14 minutes or until toothpick inserted into centers comes out clean. Cool in pans 10 minutes. Remove to wire racks; cool completely.

4. Combine pineapple with juice and cornstarch in medium saucepan; bring to a boil over medium-high heat. Cook and stir 1 minute or until thickened. Remove from heat; cool to room temperature.

5. Spoon 1 tablespoon whipped topping on each cupcake; top with 1 tablespoon pineapple mixture. Sprinkle with toasted coconut. Serve immediately or cover and refrigerate until ready to serve.

Makes 24 cupcakes

Sweet & Salty Cupcakes

1¼ cups all-purpose flour
1 cup sugar
⅓ cup unsweetened Dutch process cocoa powder
1 teaspoon baking soda
½ teaspoon baking powder
½ teaspoon salt
½ cup buttermilk
½ cup coffee
¼ cup vegetable oil
1 egg
½ teaspoon vanilla
½ cup whipping cream
1 cup semisweet chocolate chips
¾ cup honey roasted peanuts, coarsely chopped
¾ cup coarsely chopped pretzels
¼ to ½ cup caramel ice cream topping

1. Preheat oven to 350°F. Line 12 standard (2½-inch) muffin cups with paper baking cups.

2. Combine flour, sugar, cocoa, baking soda, baking powder and salt in large bowl; mix well. Whisk buttermilk, coffee, oil, egg and vanilla in medium bowl until well blended. Stir into flour mixture until well blended. Spoon evenly into prepared muffin cups.

3. Bake 15 minutes or until toothpick inserted into centers comes out clean. Cool in pan 5 minutes. Remove to wire rack; cool completely.

4. Bring cream to a simmer in small saucepan over medium heat. Place chocolate chips in medium heatproof bowl. Pour hot cream over chocolate chips; let stand 2 minutes. Whisk mixture until chocolate is melted and mixture is smooth.

Dip tops of cupcakes in chocolate mixture; return to wire rack. Let stand 10 minutes; dip tops again, if desired.

5. Sprinkle with peanuts and pretzels. Drizzle with caramel topping just before serving.   *Makes 12 cupcakes*

Tip: The pretzels and peanuts become soggy if they are sprinkled on the cupcakes too early. Prepare the cupcakes a day in advance and add the ganache and toppings the next day.

Vanilla-Strawberry Cupcakes

   2 cups all-purpose flour
   2 teaspoons baking powder
   ¼ teaspoon salt
1¾ cups granulated sugar
   ¾ cup (1½ sticks) butter, softened, divided
   ¾ cup milk
3½ teaspoons vanilla, divided
   3 egg whites
   ½ cup strawberry preserves
   1 package (8 ounces) cream cheese, chilled and cut into cubes
   2 cups powdered sugar
   1 to 1½ cups sliced fresh strawberries

1. Preheat oven to 350°F. Line 28 standard (2½-inch) muffin cups with paper baking cups.

2. Combine flour, baking powder and salt in medium bowl; mix well. Beat granulated sugar and ½ cup butter in large bowl with electric mixer at medium speed 1 minute. Add milk and 1½ teaspoons vanilla; beat at low speed 30 seconds. Gradually add flour mixture; beat at medium speed 2 minutes. Add egg whites; beat 1 minute. Spoon evenly into prepared muffin cups. Drop 1 teaspoon preserves on top of batter in each cup; swirl into batter with toothpick.

3. Bake 20 to 22 minutes or until toothpick inserted into centers comes out clean. Cool in pans 10 minutes. Remove to wire racks; cool completely.

4. Combine cream cheese, remaining ¼ cup butter and 2 teaspoons vanilla in food processor; process just until blended. Add powdered sugar; process using on/off pulsing action just until sugar is incorporated. (Do not overmix or frosting will be too soft to spread.)

5. Frost cupcakes; garnish with strawberries. Serve immediately or cover and refrigerate until ready to serve.

Makes 28 cupcakes

Red Velvet Cupcakes

2¼ cups all-purpose flour
1 teaspoon salt
2 bottles (1 ounce each) red food coloring
3 tablespoons unsweetened cocoa powder
1 cup buttermilk
1 teaspoon vanilla
1½ cups sugar
½ cup (1 stick) butter, softened
2 eggs
1 teaspoon white vinegar
1 teaspoon baking soda
1 to 2 containers (16 ounces each) whipped cream cheese frosting
Toasted coconut* (optional)

To toast coconut, spread evenly on ungreased baking sheet. Bake in preheated 350°F oven 5 to 7 minutes or until light golden brown, stirring occasionally.

1. Preheat oven to 350°F. Line 18 standard (2½-inch) muffin cups with paper baking cups.

2. Combine flour and salt in medium bowl; mix well. Gradually stir food coloring into cocoa in small bowl until smooth and well blended. Combine buttermilk and vanilla in another small bowl.

3. Beat sugar and butter in large bowl with electric mixer at medium speed 4 minutes or until light and fluffy. Add eggs, one at a time, beating well after each addition. Add cocoa mixture; beat until well blended and uniform in color. Alternately add flour mixture and buttermilk mixture, beating well after each addition. Stir vinegar into baking soda in small bowl; gently stir into batter with spatula or spoon (do not use mixer). Spoon evenly into prepared muffin cups.

4. Bake 20 minutes or until toothpick inserted into centers comes out clean. Cool in pans 10 minutes. Remove to wire racks; cool completely.

5. Frost cupcakes; sprinkle with toasted coconut.

Makes 18 cupcakes

German Chocolate Cupcakes

1 package (about 18 ounces) German chocolate cake mix, plus ingredients
    to prepare mix
1 can (12 ounces) evaporated milk
¾ cup granulated sugar
½ cup (1 stick) butter, softened
4 egg yolks, beaten
¼ cup packed brown sugar
2 cups shredded coconut
1 cup chopped pecans
3 ounces semisweet chocolate, finely chopped

1. Preheat oven to 350°F. Line 22 standard (2½-inch) muffin cups with paper baking cups.

2. Prepare cake mix according to package directions. Spoon batter evenly into prepared muffin cups.

3. Bake 20 minutes or until toothpick inserted into centers comes out clean. Cool in pans 10 minutes. Remove to wire racks; cool completely.

4. Combine evaporated milk, granulated sugar, butter, egg yolks and brown sugar in medium saucepan. Cook over medium-low heat 8 to 10 minutes or until slightly thickened and mixture just begins to bubble, stirring constantly. Stir in coconut and pecans. Remove from heat; let stand 1 hour or until thickened, stirring occasionally.

5. Spoon cooled coconut mixture evenly over cupcakes.

6. Microwave chocolate in small microwavable bowl on HIGH 30 seconds; stir. Microwave at additional 15-second intervals until chocolate is melted. Drizzle over cupcakes. Let stand until set. *Makes 22 cupcakes*

Butter Pecan Cupcakes

  3 cups all-purpose flour
  2 teaspoons baking powder
  ½ teaspoon salt
  2 cups granulated sugar
  1 cup (2 sticks) butter, softened
  4 eggs
  ¾ cup milk
  ¼ cup canola or vegetable oil
1½ teaspoons vanilla
  2 cups chopped pecans, toasted*
    Browned Butter Frosting (page 23)
    Whole pecans (optional)

To toast pecans, spread in single layer on baking sheet. Bake in preheated 350°F oven 5 to 7 minutes or until fragrant, stirring frequently.

1. Preheat oven to 350°F. Line 30 standard (2½-inch) muffin cups with paper baking cups.

2. Combine flour, baking powder and salt in medium bowl; mix well. Beat sugar and butter in large bowl with electric mixer at medium speed until creamy. Add eggs, one at a time, beating well after each addition. Combine milk, oil and vanilla in small bowl; mix well. Alternately add flour mixture and milk mixture, beating well after each addition. Stir in chopped pecans. Spoon evenly into prepared muffin cups.

3. Bake 20 minutes or until toothpick inserted into centers comes out clean. Cool in pans 10 minutes. Remove to wire racks; cool completely.

4. Prepare Browned Butter Frosting. Frost cupcakes; garnish with whole pecans.

Makes 30 cupcakes

Browned Butter Frosting: Melt 1 cup (2 sticks) butter in small saucepan over medium heat. Cook and stir until light brown. Remove from heat; let stand 10 minutes. Combine browned butter, 5½ cups powdered sugar, ¼ cup milk, 1½ teaspoons vanilla and ⅛ teaspoon salt in large bowl. Beat with electric mixer at medium speed until smooth. Add additional milk, 1 tablespoon at a time, if frosting is too stiff.

Classic Chocolate Cupcakes

1¾ cups all-purpose flour
1¼ cups sugar
  2 teaspoons baking powder
  ½ teaspoon salt
  ¾ cup vegetable oil
  ¾ cup milk
  3 eggs
1½ teaspoons vanilla
  8 squares (1 ounce each) semisweet chocolate, melted and cooled slightly
    Chocolate Buttercream Frosting (page 25)
    Colored sprinkles

1. Preheat oven to 350°F. Line 20 standard (2½-inch) muffin cups with paper baking cups.

2. Combine flour, sugar, baking powder and salt in large bowl; mix well. Add oil, milk, eggs and vanilla; beat with electric mixer at medium speed 2 minutes or until well blended. Stir in melted chocolate until well blended. Spoon evenly into prepared muffin cups.

3. Bake 25 minutes or until toothpick inserted into centers comes out clean. Cool in pans 10 minutes. Remove to wire racks; cool completely.

4. Prepare Chocolate Buttercream Frosting. Frost cupcakes; decorate with sprinkles.

Makes 20 cupcakes

Chocolate Buttercream Frosting

4 cups powdered sugar, sifted, divided
¾ cup (1½ sticks) butter, softened
**6 squares (1 ounce each) unsweetened chocolate, melted and
    cooled slightly**
4 to 8 tablespoons milk, divided
¾ teaspoon vanilla

Beat 2 cups powdered sugar, butter, melted chocolate, 4 tablespoons milk and vanilla in large bowl with electric mixer at medium speed until smooth. Add remaining 2 cups powdered sugar; beat until light and fluffy, adding more milk, 1 tablespoon at a time, if necessary, to reach desired spreading consistency. *Makes about 3 cups*

Cream-Filled Cupcakes

    1 package (about 18 ounces) dark chocolate cake mix, plus ingredients
        to prepare mix
 ½ cup (1 stick) butter, softened
 ¼ cup shortening
    3 cups powdered sugar
1⅓ cups whipping cream, divided
    1 teaspoon salt
    2 cups semisweet chocolate chips

1. Preheat oven to 350°F. Line 24 standard (2½-inch) muffin cups with paper baking cups.

2. Prepare cake mix according to package directions. Spoon batter evenly into prepared muffin cups.

3. Bake 20 minutes or until toothpick inserted into centers comes out clean. Cool in pans 10 minutes. Remove to wire racks; cool completely.

4. Beat butter and shortening in large bowl with electric mixer at medium speed until well blended. Add powdered sugar, ⅓ cup cream and salt; beat at low speed 1 minute. Beat at medium-high speed 2 minutes or until fluffy.

5. Place filling in piping bag fitted with large round tip. Insert tip into tops of cupcakes; squeeze bag gently to fill centers. Reserve remaining filling.

6. Bring remaining 1 cup cream to a simmer in small saucepan over medium heat. Place chocolate chips in medium heatproof bowl. Pour hot cream over chocolate chips; let stand 2 minutes. Whisk mixture until chocolate is melted and mixture is smooth. Dip tops of cupcakes in chocolate mixture; return to wire racks. Let stand 10 minutes; dip tops again, if desired. Let stand until set.

7. Pipe swirl design on top of chocolate with reserved filling.

Makes 24 cupcakes

Peanut Butter Cupcakes

 2 cups all-purpose flour
 2 teaspoons baking powder
½ teaspoon baking soda
½ teaspoon salt
 1 cup creamy peanut butter, divided
¼ cup (½ stick) butter, softened
 1 cup packed light brown sugar
 2 eggs
 1 cup milk
1½ cups mini semisweet chocolate chips, divided, plus additional for garnish
    Peanut Buttery Frosting (page 29)

1. Preheat oven to 350°F. Line 24 standard (2½-inch) muffin cups with paper baking cups.

2. Combine flour, baking powder, baking soda and salt in small bowl; mix well. Beat ½ cup peanut butter and butter in large bowl with electric mixer at medium speed until well blended. Add brown sugar; beat until well blended. Add eggs, one at a time, beating well after each addition. Alternately add flour mixture and milk, beating well after each addition. Stir in 1 cup chocolate chips. Spoon evenly into prepared muffin cups.

3. Bake 15 minutes or until toothpick inserted into centers comes out clean. Cool completely in pans on wire racks.

4. Prepare Peanut Buttery Frosting. Frost cupcakes.

5. Place remaining ½ cup peanut butter in small microwavable bowl. Microwave on HIGH 15 seconds or until melted. Place remaining ½ cup chocolate chips in another small microwavable bowl. Microwave on HIGH 15 seconds or until melted. Drizzle peanut butter and chocolate over frosting. Garnish with additional chocolate chips.

Makes 24 cupcakes

Peanut Buttery Frosting: Beat ½ cup (1 stick) softened butter and ½ cup creamy peanut butter in medium bowl with electric mixer at medium speed until smooth. Gradually add 2 cups sifted powdered sugar and ½ teaspoon vanilla until blended. Add 3 to 6 tablespoons milk, 1 tablespoon at a time, until smooth.

Lemon Poppy Seed Cupcakes

1½ packages (12 ounces) cream cheese, softened
1½ cups plus ⅓ cup powdered sugar, divided
1 package (about 18 ounces) lemon cake mix, plus ingredients to prepare mix
1 tablespoon poppy seeds
Grated peel and juice of 1 lemon
Candied violets (optional)

1. Preheat oven to 350°F. Line 18 standard (2½-inch) muffin cups with paper baking cups.

2. Beat cream cheese and ⅓ cup powdered sugar in medium bowl with electric mixer at medium speed 1 minute or until light and fluffy.

3. Prepare cake mix according to package directions; stir in poppy seeds. Spoon 2 tablespoons batter into each prepared muffin cup. Place 2 teaspoons cream cheese mixture in center of each cup; top with 2 tablespoons batter.

4. Bake 22 to 24 minutes. Cool in pans 10 minutes. Remove to wire racks; cool completely.

5. Whisk remaining 1½ cups powdered sugar, lemon peel and lemon juice in small bowl until smooth. Dip tops of cupcakes into glaze. Top with candied violets, if desired.   *Makes 18 cupcakes*

Black & Whites

**1 package (about 18 ounces) vanilla cake mix, plus ingredients
to prepare mix**
⅔ cup semisweet chocolate chips, melted
4 ounces cream cheese, softened
1 cup prepared vanilla frosting
1 cup prepared chocolate frosting

1. Preheat oven to 350°F. Line 24 standard (2½-inch) muffin cups with paper baking cups.

2. Prepare cake mix according to package directions. Transfer half of batter (about 2½ cups) to medium bowl. Add melted chocolate and cream cheese to remaining batter; beat with electric mixer at medium speed 2 minutes or until smooth and well blended.

3. Spoon chocolate and vanilla batters evenly side by side into prepared muffin cups. (Use chocolate batter first as it is slightly thicker and easier to position on one side of muffin cups.)

4. Bake 15 minutes or until toothpick inserted into centers comes out clean. Cool in pans 10 minutes. Remove to wire racks; cool completely.

5. Spread vanilla frosting over half of each cupcake; spread chocolate frosting over remaining half of each cupcake.   *Makes 24 cupcakes*

Chocolate Indulgences

Café Mocha Cupcakes

2 tablespoons plus 2 teaspoons instant coffee granules, divided
1⅓ cups plus 1 tablespoon water, divided
1 package (about 18 ounces) devil's food cake mix
3 eggs
⅓ cup canola oil
1 container (8 ounces) frozen whipped topping, thawed
Cocoa powder

1. Preheat oven to 350°F. Line 24 standard (2½-inch) muffin cups with paper baking cups.

2. Whisk 2 tablespoons coffee granules in 1⅓ cups water in large bowl until dissolved. Add cake mix, eggs and oil; beat with electric mixer at low speed 30 seconds. Beat at medium speed 2 minutes, scraping bowl occasionally. Spoon batter evenly into prepared muffin cups.

3. Bake 15 to 20 minutes or until toothpick inserted into centers comes out clean. Remove to wire racks; cool completely.

4. Whisk remaining 2 teaspoons coffee granules and in 1 tablespoon water in small cup until dissolved. Stir coffee mixture into whipped topping until well blended.

5. Frost cupcakes; sprinkle with cocoa. Serve immediately or cover and refrigerate until ready to serve. *Makes 24 servings*

Dark Chocolate Banana Cupcakes

1½ cups all-purpose flour
1½ cups granulated sugar
½ cup unsweetened Dutch process cocoa powder
2 tablespoons packed brown sugar
2 teaspoons baking powder
½ teaspoon salt
½ cup vegetable oil
2 eggs
¼ cup buttermilk
1 teaspoon vanilla
2 bananas, mashed (about 1 cup)
1½ cups whipping cream
2 cups dark chocolate chips
Dried banana chips

1. Preheat oven to 350°F. Line 18 standard (2½-inch) muffin cups with paper baking cups.

2. Combine flour, granulated sugar, cocoa, brown sugar, baking powder and salt in large bowl; mix well. Add oil, eggs, buttermilk and vanilla; beat with electric mixer at medium speed 2 minutes or until well blended. Add bananas; beat until well blended. Spoon evenly into prepared muffin cups.

3. Bake 25 minutes or until toothpick inserted into centers comes out clean. Cool in pans 10 minutes. Remove to wire racks; cool completely.

4. Bring cream to a simmer in small saucepan over medium heat. Place chocolate chips in medium heatproof bowl. Pour hot cream over chocolate chips; let stand 2 minutes. Whisk mixture until chocolate is melted and mixture is smooth. Dip tops of cupcakes in chocolate mixture; return to wire racks. Let stand 10 minutes; dip tops again, if desired.

5. Drizzle banana chips with remaining chocolate mixture; place on cupcakes.

Makes 18 cupcakes

Chocolate COCA-COLA® Cupcakes With Cherries

1 package dark chocolate cake mix
  Eggs and oil, per cake mix instructions
1 can COCA-COLA®
1 jar (8 ounces) maraschino cherries in syrup
1 can (21 ounces) cherry pie filling, lightly drained
  Cherry Butter Cream Frosting (recipe follows)

Prepare cake mix according to package directions, substituting COCA-COLA for water.

Add maraschino cherry syrup and cherry pie filling.

Line muffin cups with paper baking cups. Pour batter into cups and bake according to directions for cupcakes.

Cool completely; frost with Cherry Butter Cream Frosting and top each with a maraschino cherry. *Makes 27 cupcakes*

Cherry Butter Cream Frosting

5½ tablespoons butter, softened
2 tablespoons cream cheese, softened
2½ cups confectioners sugar
2 tablespoons maraschino cherry syrup

Using an electric mixer, beat together butter, cream cheese and sugar in medium bowl until fluffy, about 1 minute.

Add cherry syrup and beat until combined and creamy.

Rayna's Nutty Marshmallow-Topped Chocolate Cupcakes

1 box (18 ounces) chocolate cake mix
1 cup HELLMANN'S® or BEST FOODS® Real Mayonnaise
1 cup water
3 eggs
½ cup SKIPPY® Creamy Peanut Butter
2 jars (7½ ounces each) marshmallow creme
1 cup frozen whipped topping, thawed
Chocolate sprinkles or other cake decorations (optional)

1. Preheat oven to 350°F. Line two 12-cup muffin pans with cupcake liners; set aside.

2. Beat cake mix, HELLMANN'S® or BEST FOODS® Real Mayonnaise, water and eggs in large bowl with electric mixer on low speed 30 seconds. Beat on medium speed, scraping sides occasionally, 2 minutes. Evenly pour into prepared pans.

3. Bake 18 minutes or until toothpick inserted in centers comes out clean. Cool 10 minutes on wire racks; remove from pans and cool completely.

4. Meanwhile, whisk together SKIPPY® Creamy Peanut Butter, marshmallow creme and whipped topping in medium bowl. Frost cupcakes with peanut butter frosting. Decorate as desired. *Makes 24 servings*

Tip: Cake batter can also be baked in two 9-inch or one 13×9-inch cake pan and then frosted!

Prep Time: 15 minutes • **Cook Time:** 18 minutes

Gooey Coconut Chocolate Cupcakes

1 package (about 18 ounces) chocolate cake mix, plus ingredients to prepare mix
½ cup (1 stick) butter
1 cup packed brown sugar
⅓ cup whipping cream
1½ cups sweetened flaked coconut
½ cup chopped pecans

1. Preheat oven to 350°F. Line 24 standard (2½-inch) muffin cups with paper baking cups.

2. Prepare cake mix according to package directions. Spoon batter evenly into prepared muffin cups.

3. Bake 18 minutes or until toothpick inserted into centers comes out clean. Do not remove cupcakes from pans.

4. Melt butter in medium saucepan over low heat. Stir in brown sugar and cream until well blended and sugar is dissolved. Add coconut and pecans; mix well. Spread 2 to 3 tablespoons over each cupcake.

5. Preheat broiler. Broil cupcakes 2 to 3 minutes or until tops begin to brown and edges bubble. Serve warm or at room temperature. *Makes 24 cupcakes*

Chocolate Tiramisu Cupcakes

Cupcakes

- **1 package (about 18 ounces) chocolate cake mix**
- **1¼ cups water**
- **3 eggs**
- **⅓ cup melted butter or vegetable oil**
- **2 tablespoons instant espresso powder**
- **2 tablespoons brandy (optional)**

Frosting

- **1 package (8 ounces) cream cheese or mascarpone cheese, softened**
- **1½ to 1¾ cups powdered sugar**
- **2 tablespoons coffee-flavored liqueur (optional)**
- **1 tablespoon unsweetened cocoa powder**

1. Preheat oven to 350°F. Line 30 standard (2½-inch) muffin cups with paper baking cups.

2. Beat cake mix, water, eggs, butter, espresso powder and brandy, if desired, in large bowl with electric mixer at low speed 30 seconds. Beat at medium speed 2 minutes. Spoon evenly into prepared muffin cups.

3. Bake 20 minutes or until toothpick inserted into centers comes out clean. Cool in pans 10 minutes. Remove to wire racks; cool completely.

4. Beat cream cheese and 1½ cups powdered sugar in large bowl with electric mixer at medium speed until well blended. Add liqueur, if desired; beat until well blended. If frosting is too soft, beat in additional powdered sugar or chill until desired spreading consistency is reached.

5. Frost cupcakes; sprinkle with cocoa. Store at room temperature up to 24 hours or cover and refrigerate up to 3 days. *Makes 30 cupcakes*

White Chocolate Macadamia Cupcakes

1 package (about 18 ounces) white cake mix *without* pudding in the mix, plus ingredients to prepare mix
1 package (4-serving size) white chocolate instant pudding and pie filling mix
¾ cup chopped macadamia nuts
1 cup white chocolate chips
1 container (16 ounces) white frosting
1½ cups sweetened flaked coconut, toasted*

*To toast coconut, spread evenly on ungreased baking sheet. Bake in preheated 350°F oven 5 to 7 minutes or until light golden brown, stirring occasionally.

1. Preheat oven to 350°F. Line 22 standard (2½-inch) muffin cups with paper baking cups.

2. Prepare cake mix according to package directions; stir in pudding mix. Stir in macadamia nuts. Spoon batter evenly into prepared muffin cups.

3. Bake 20 minutes or until toothpick inserted into centers comes out clean. Cool in pans 10 minutes. Remove to wire racks; cool completely.

4. Microwave white chocolate chips in small microwavable bowl on MEDIUM (50%) 2 minutes or until melted and smooth, stirring at 30-second intervals. Cool slightly; stir into frosting.

5. Frost cupcakes; top with toasted coconut.

Makes 22 cupcakes

Chocolate Hazelnut Cupcakes

1¾ cups all-purpose flour
1½ teaspoons baking powder
½ teaspoon salt
2 cups chocolate hazelnut spread, divided
⅓ cup (⅔ stick) butter, softened
¾ cup sugar
2 eggs
1 teaspoon vanilla
1¼ cups milk
Chopped hazelnuts (optional)

1. Preheat oven to 350°F. Line 18 standard (2½-inch) muffin cups with paper cups.

2. Combine flour, baking powder and salt in medium bowl; mix well. Beat ⅓ cup chocolate hazelnut spread and butter in large bowl with electric mixer at medium speed until smooth. Add sugar; beat until well blended. Add eggs and vanilla; beat until well blended. Alternately add flour mixture and milk, beating well after each addition. Spoon evenly into prepared muffin cups.

3. Bake 20 minutes or until toothpick inserted into centers comes out clean. Cool in pans 10 minutes. Remove to wire racks; cool completely.

4. Frost cupcakes with remaining 1⅔ cups chocolate hazelnut spread; sprinkle with hazelnuts, if desired. *Makes 18 cupcakes*

Chocolate Chip Cookie Cupcakes

1 package (about 18 ounces) yellow cake mix, plus ingredients to prepare mix
1½ cups semisweet chocolate chips, divided
1½ cups chopped walnuts or pecans, divided
1 container (16 ounces) cream cheese frosting
¾ cup creamy peanut butter

1. Preheat oven to 350°F. Line 24 standard (2½-inch) muffin cups with paper baking cups.

2. Prepare cake mix according to package directions. Stir in ¾ cup chocolate chips and ¾ cup walnuts. Spoon batter evenly into prepared muffin cups.

3. Bake 20 minutes or until toothpick inserted into centers comes out clean. Cool in pans 10 minutes. Remove to wire racks; cool completely.

4. Stir frosting and peanut butter in medium bowl until well blended.

5. Frost cupcakes; sprinkle with remaining ¾ cup chocolate chips and ¾ cup walnuts. *Makes 24 cupcakes*

Bittersweet Chocolate Raspberry Cupcakes

1½ cups all-purpose flour
 1 teaspoon baking soda
 1 teaspoon baking powder
½ teaspoon salt
¾ cup hot coffee
¾ cup unsweetened cocoa powder
 8 squares (8 ounces) bittersweet chocolate, chopped, divided
1¼ cups sugar
 2 eggs
⅓ cup vegetable oil
 1 teaspoon vanilla
¾ cup buttermilk
 2 pints fresh raspberries, divided
½ cup whipping cream

1. Preheat oven to 350°F. Line 20 standard (2½-inch) muffin cups with paper baking cups.

2. Combine flour, baking soda, baking powder and salt in small bowl; mix well. Whisk coffee, cocoa and 2 ounces chopped chocolate in large bowl until chocolate is melted and mixture is smooth. Stir in sugar, eggs, oil and vanilla until well blended. Alternately add flour mixture and buttermilk, beating well after each addition. Spoon evenly into prepared muffin cups. Place 3 raspberries in each cup.

3. Bake 20 minutes or until toothpick inserted into centers comes out clean. Cool in pans 5 minutes. Remove to wire racks; cool completely.

4. Bring cream to a simmer in small saucepan over medium heat. Place remaining 6 ounces chopped chocolate in medium heatproof bowl. Pour hot cream over chocolate; let stand 2 minutes. Whisk mixture until chocolate is melted and mixture is smooth. Dip tops of cupcakes in chocolate mixture; return to wire racks. Let stand 10 minutes; dip tops again, if desired. Top with raspberries. Let stand until set.

Makes 20 cupcakes

Triple Treat Chocolate Cupcakes

1 package (18.25 ounces) devil's food cake mix
1 package (3.9 ounces) chocolate instant pudding and pie filling mix
1 container (8 ounces) sour cream
4 large eggs
½ cup vegetable oil
½ cup warm water
1⅔ cups (10-ounce package) **NESTLÉ® TOLL HOUSE® SWIRLED™**
    Semi-Sweet Chocolate & Premier White Morsels, *divided*
1 container (16 ounces) prepared white frosting

PREHEAT oven to 350°F. Paper-line 30 muffin cups.

COMBINE cake mix, pudding mix, sour cream, eggs, vegetable oil and water in large mixer bowl; beat on low speed until just blended. Beat on medium speed for 2 minutes. Stir in *1 cup* morsels. Fill each cup two-thirds full.

BAKE for 25 to 28 minutes or until wooden pick inserted in center comes out clean. Cool in pans for 10 minutes; remove to wire racks to cool completely. Frost; decorate with *remaining ⅔ cup* morsels.   *Makes 2½ dozen cupcakes*

Prep Time: 20 minutes • **Baking Time:** 25 minutes • **Cooling Time:** 10 minutes

Peanut Butter & Milk Chocolate Cupcakes

1 package (about 18 ounces) butter recipe yellow cake mix
½ cup creamy peanut butter
½ cup (1 stick) butter, softened, divided
3 eggs
¼ cup water
2 bars (3½ ounces each) milk chocolate, broken into small pieces
¼ cup whipping cream
Dash salt
Peanut butter chips

1. Preheat oven to 350°F. Line 24 standard (2½-inch) muffin cups with paper baking cups.

2. Beat cake mix, peanut butter, ¼ cup butter, eggs and water in large bowl with electric mixer at low speed 30 seconds or until moistened. Beat at medium speed 2 minutes. Spoon evenly into prepared muffin cups.

3. Bake 24 minutes or until toothpick inserted into centers comes out clean. Cool in pans 10 minutes. Remove to wire racks; cool completely.

4. Combine chocolate, remaining ¼ cup butter, cream and salt in small heavy saucepan. Heat over low heat until butter and chocolate are melted and mixture is smooth, stirring constantly. (Mixture should be warm, not hot.) Immediately spoon about 1 tablespoon chocolate glaze over each cupcake, spreading to cover top. Sprinkle with peanut butter chips. *Makes 24 cupcakes*

Spicy Chocolate Cupcakes

2½ cups all-purpose flour
1 teaspoon baking soda
1 teaspoon baking powder
1 teaspoon ground cinnamon
½ teaspoon salt
⅛ teaspoon ground nutmeg
1½ cups sugar
¾ cup (1½ sticks) butter, softened
3 eggs
1½ teaspoons vanilla
1 container (7 ounces) plain Greek yogurt
2 tablespoons canola or vegetable oil
Spicy Chocolate Frosting (page 59)
Chocolate curls (optional)

1. Preheat oven to 350°F. Line 24 standard (2½-inch) muffin cups with paper baking cups.

2. Combine flour, baking soda, baking powder, cinnamon, salt and nutmeg in medium bowl; mix well. Beat sugar and butter in large bowl with electric mixer at medium speed until creamy. Add eggs and vanilla; beat until well blended. Alternately add flour mixture, yogurt and oil, beating well after each addition. Spoon evenly into prepared muffin cups.

3. Bake 18 minutes or until toothpick inserted into centers comes out clean. Cool in pans 10 minutes. Remove to wire racks; cool completely.

4. Prepare Spicy Chocolate Frosting. Frost cupcakes; garnish with chocolate curls.

Makes 24 cupcakes

Spicy Chocolate Frosting: Beat 2 cups (4 sticks) softened butter in large bowl with electric mixer at medium speed until creamy. Add 4 cups powdered sugar, ¼ cup milk, 1 teaspoon ground cinnamon, 1 teaspoon ancho chile powder, 1 teaspoon vanilla and ½ teaspoon ground red pepper; beat until fluffy. Beat in 10 squares (10 ounces) cooled melted bittersweet chocolate until blended.

Chocolate Indulgences • 59

Polka Dot Pumpkin Cupcakes

Topping
- ½ cup (4 ounces) cream cheese, softened
- 1 large egg
- 2 tablespoons granulated sugar
- ⅔ cup NESTLÉ® TOLL HOUSE® Semi-Sweet Chocolate Mini Morsels

Cupcakes
- 1 package (16 ounces) pound cake mix
- 1 cup LIBBY'S® 100% Pure Pumpkin
- ⅓ cup water
- 2 large eggs
- 2 teaspoons pumpkin pie spice
- 1 teaspoon baking soda

PREHEAT oven to 325°F. Grease or paper-line 18 muffin cups.

For Topping

BEAT cream cheese, egg and granulated sugar in small mixer bowl until smooth. Stir in morsels.

For Cupcakes

COMBINE cake mix, pumpkin, water, eggs, pumpkin pie spice and baking soda in large mixer bowl; beat on medium speed for 3 minutes. Pour batter into prepared muffin cups, filling three fourths full. Spoon about 1 tablespoon topping over batter.

BAKE for 25 to 30 minutes or until wooden pick inserted in center comes out clean. Cool in pans on wire racks for 10 minutes; remove to wire racks to cool completely.

Makes 1½ dozen cupcakes

Prep Time: 15 minutes • **Baking Time:** 25 minutes • **Cooling Time:** 10 minutes

Chocolate Malt Cupcakes

1 package (about 18 ounces) milk chocolate cake mix with pudding in the mix
2 cups (1 pint) chocolate ice cream, softened
3 eggs
¾ cup water
½ cup chocolate malted milk powder*
1 container (16 ounces) milk chocolate frosting
32 malted milk balls

You can find malted milk powder in the supermarket with the ice cream toppings or in the powdered beverage aisle.

1. Preheat oven to 350°F. Line 32 standard (2½-inch) muffin cups with paper baking cups.

2. Beat cake mix, ice cream, eggs, water and malted milk powder in large bowl with electric mixer at low speed 30 seconds. Beat at medium speed 2 minutes or until well blended. Spoon evenly into prepared muffin cups.

3. Bake 20 to 23 minutes or until toothpick inserted into centers comes out clean. Cool in pans 5 minutes. Remove to wire racks; cool completely.

4. Frost cupcakes; top with malted milk balls. *Makes 32 cupcakes*

Fun Flavors

Rocky Road Cupcakes

1 package (about 18 ounces) chocolate fudge cake mix
1⅓ cups water
3 eggs
½ cup vegetable oil
¾ cup mini semisweet chocolate chips, divided
1 container (16 ounces) chocolate frosting
1 cup mini marshmallows
⅔ cup walnut pieces
Hot fudge ice cream topping or chocolate syrup, warmed

1. Preheat oven to 325°F. Line 22 standard (2½-inch) muffin cups with paper baking cups.

2. Beat cake mix, water, eggs, oil and ¼ cup chocolate chips in large bowl with electric mixer at low speed 30 seconds. Beat at medium speed 2 minutes or until well blended. Spoon evenly into prepared muffin cups.

3. Bake 20 minutes or until toothpick inserted into centers comes out clean. Cool in pans 10 minutes. Remove to wire racks; cool completely.

4. Frost cupcakes; top with marshmallows, walnuts and remaining ½ cup chocolate chips, pressing to adhere. Drizzle with hot fudge topping. *Makes 22 cupcakes*

Cannoli Cupcakes

2 cups all-purpose flour
½ teaspoon baking soda
½ teaspoon baking powder
½ teaspoon salt
1 cup granulated sugar
½ cup (1 stick) butter, softened
1 cup whole-milk ricotta cheese
1 teaspoon grated orange peel
1 egg
2 teaspoons vanilla, divided
1 cup whipping cream
8 ounces mascarpone cheese, softened
½ cup powdered sugar
    Mini semisweet chocolate chips and chopped unsalted pistachios

1. Preheat oven to 350°F. Line 15 standard (2½-inch) muffin cups with paper baking cups.

2. Combine flour, baking soda, baking powder and salt in small bowl; mix well. Beat granulated sugar and butter in large bowl with electric mixer at medium speed until creamy. Add ricotta cheese and orange peel; beat until blended. Add egg and 1 teaspoon vanilla; beat until well blended. Add flour mixture; beat until well blended. Spoon evenly into prepared muffin cups.

3. Bake 20 minutes or until toothpick inserted into centers comes out clean. Cool in pans 10 minutes. Remove to wire racks; cool completely.

4. Beat cream in medium bowl with electric mixer at high speed until stiff peaks form. Combine mascarpone cheese, powdered sugar and remaining 1 teaspoon vanilla in separate medium bowl. Fold in whipped cream until well blended.

5. Frost cupcakes; sprinkle with chocolate chips and pistachios.

Makes 15 cupcakes

Blueberry Cupcakes with Goat Cheese Frosting

Cupcakes
  1½ cups all-purpose flour
  1¾ teaspoons baking powder
  ½ teaspoon salt
  ½ cup granulated sugar
  ½ cup (1 stick) butter, softened
  2 eggs
  2 teaspoons vanilla
  ½ cup milk
  1 cup fresh blueberries, plus additional for garnish

Frosting
  4 ounces goat cheese
  ¼ cup (½ stick) butter, softened
  2 cups powdered sugar
  2 tablespoons milk

1. Preheat oven to 350°F. Line 12 standard (2½-inch) muffin cups with paper baking cups.

2. Combine flour, baking powder and salt in small bowl; mix well. Beat granulated sugar and ½ cup butter in large bowl with electric mixer at medium speed until light and fluffy. Add eggs and vanilla; beat until well blended. Add flour mixture and ½ cup milk; beat at low speed just until combined. Stir in 1 cup blueberries. Spoon evenly into prepared muffin cups.

3. Bake 20 minutes or until toothpick inserted into centers comes out clean. Cool in pan 10 minutes. Remove to wire rack; cool completely.

4. Beat goat cheese and ¼ cup butter in large bowl with electric mixer at medium speed until well blended. Add powdered sugar and 2 tablespoons milk; beat until smooth.

5. Frost cupcakes; garnish with additional blueberries.   *Makes 12 cupcakes*

Apple Cheddar Cupcakes

Cheddar Streusel Topping (recipe follows)
1 cup all-purpose flour
½ teaspoon baking powder
½ teaspoon baking soda
½ teaspoon salt
6 tablespoons butter, softened
½ cup granulated sugar
¼ cup packed brown sugar
1 egg
1 teaspoon vanilla
½ cup milk
1 cup finely chopped peeled Granny Smith apple
½ cup (2 ounces) finely shredded sharp Cheddar cheese

1. Preheat oven to 350°F. Line 36 mini (1¾-inch) muffin cups with paper baking cups. Prepare Cheddar Streusel Topping.

2. Combine flour, baking powder, baking soda and salt in small bowl; mix well. Beat butter, granulated sugar and brown sugar in large bowl with electric mixer at medium speed until creamy. Add egg and vanilla; beat until well blended. Add flour mixture and milk; stir just until combined. Stir in apple and cheese. Spoon evenly into prepared muffin cups. Sprinkle evenly with Cheddar Streusel Topping.

3. Bake 15 minutes or until toothpick inserted into centers comes out clean. Cool in pans 5 minutes. Remove to wire racks; serve warm or at room temperature.

Makes 36 mini cupcakes

Cheddar Streusel Topping: Combine ⅓ cup all-purpose flour, 2 tablespoons finely shredded sharp Cheddar cheese, 2 tablespoons melted butter and 1 tablespoon granulated sugar in medium bowl; stir with fork until small crumbs form.

Margarita Cupcakes

1 package (about 18 ounces) white cake mix
¾ cup plus 2 tablespoons margarita mix, divided
2 eggs
⅓ cup vegetable oil
¼ cup water
3 teaspoons grated lime peel, divided
Juice of 1 lime
2 tablespoons tequila or lime juice
3 cups powdered sugar
1 tablespoon white decorating sugar
1 tablespoon salt
Green and yellow food coloring
Lime peel strips (optional)

1. Preheat oven to 350°F. Line 24 standard (2½-inch) muffin cups with paper baking cups.

2. Stir cake mix, ¾ cup margarita mix, eggs, oil, water, 1 teaspoon lime peel and lime juice in large bowl until well blended. Spoon evenly into prepared muffin cups.

3. Bake 20 minutes or until toothpick inserted into centers comes out clean. Cool in pans 10 minutes. Remove to wire racks; cool completely.

4. Combine tequila, remaining 2 tablespoons margarita mix and 2 teaspoons lime peel in medium bowl. Gradually whisk in powdered sugar. Combine decorating sugar and salt in small bowl. Add food coloring, one drop at a time, until desired shade is reached.

5. Spread glaze over cupcakes; dip edges in sugar-salt mixture. Garnish with lime peel strips. *Makes 24 cupcakes*

Orange Dreamsicle Cupcakes

3 cups all-purpose flour
3 envelopes (0.15-ounces each) orange unsweetened drink mix
4 teaspoons baking powder
¼ teaspoon salt
2 cups granulated sugar
2 cups (4 sticks) butter, softened, divided
4 eggs
1 cup plus 6 tablespoons milk, divided
3 teaspoons vanilla, divided
6 cups powdered sugar
  Orange food coloring
  White sprinkles

1. Preheat oven to 350°F. Line 24 standard (2½-inch) muffin cups with paper baking cups.

2. Combine flour, drink mix, baking powder and salt in small bowl; mix well. Beat granulated sugar and 1 cup butter in large bowl with electric mixer at medium speed until creamy. Add eggs, one at a time, beating well after each addition. Add flour mixture; beat until well blended. Add 1 cup milk and 2 teaspoons vanilla; beat until smooth. Spoon evenly into prepared muffin cups.

3. Bake 20 minutes or until toothpick inserted into centers comes out clean. Cool in pans 10 minutes. Remove to wire racks; cool completely.

4. Beat powdered sugar, remaining 1 cup butter, 6 tablespoons milk and 1 teaspoon vanilla in large bowl with electric mixer at medium speed until fluffy. Add food coloring, a few drops at a time, until desired shade is reached.

5. Frost cupcakes; top with sprinkles.

Makes 24 cupcakes

Pistachio-Chocolate Chip Cupcakes

 2 cups all-purpose flour
1½ cups sugar
 4 teaspoons baking powder
 ½ teaspoon salt
 ½ cup (1 stick) butter, softened
 1 cup milk
 1 teaspoon vanilla
 3 eggs
 1 cup chopped pistachios, plus additional for garnish
 1 cup mini semisweet chocolate chips
 2 containers (16 ounces each) vanilla frosting
 ¾ cup marshmallow creme
   Green gel food coloring

1. Preheat oven to 350°F. Line 24 standard (2½-inch) muffin cups with paper baking cups.

2. Combine flour, sugar, baking powder and salt in large bowl; mix well. Add butter; beat with electric mixer at medium speed 30 seconds. Add milk and vanilla; beat 2 minutes. Add eggs; beat 2 minutes. Stir in 1 cup pistachios and chocolate chips. Spoon evenly into prepared muffin cups.

3. Bake 20 minutes or until toothpick inserted into centers comes out clean. Cool in pans 10 minutes. Remove to wire racks; cool completely.

4. Stir frosting, marshmallow creme and food coloring in medium bowl until blended.

5. Frost cupcakes; sprinkle with additional pistachios.   *Makes 24 cupcakes*

Pumpkin Carrot Cupcakes with Orange-Cream Cheese Frosting

- **1 cup whole-wheat flour**
- **1 cup all-purpose flour**
- **2 teaspoons ground cinnamon**
- **2 teaspoons baking soda**
- **1 teaspoon salt**
- **2 cups packed brown sugar**
- **½ cup vegetable oil**
- **3 teaspoons grated orange peel,** *divided*
- **1 can (15 ounces) LIBBY'S® 100% Pure Pumpkin**
- **4 large eggs**
- **2 cups grated carrots**
- **¾ cup golden raisins**
- **4 ounces light cream cheese**
- **1 tablespoon butter, softened**
- **1½ cups powdered sugar, sifted**
- **Candied orange peel for garnish (optional)**

PREHEAT oven to 350°F. Paper-line 24 muffin cups.

COMBINE whole-wheat flour, all-purpose flour, cinnamon, baking soda and salt in medium bowl. Beat brown sugar, oil and *2 teaspoons* grated orange peel in large mixer bowl until blended. Add pumpkin and eggs; beat well. Gradually beat in flour mixture. Fold in carrots and raisins. Spoon batter into prepared muffin cups, filling ⅔ full.

BAKE for 25 minutes or until wooden pick inserted in cupcake comes out almost clean. Cool in pans on wire racks for 10 minutes; remove to wire racks to cool completely.

BEAT cream cheese, butter, powdered sugar and *remaining 1 teaspoon* grated orange peel in small mixer bowl until smooth. Spread over cupcakes; garnish with candied orange peel. *Makes 2 dozen cupcakes*

Prep Time: 25 minutes • **Cooking Time:** 25 minutes • **Cooling Time:** 20 minutes

Iced Coffee Cupcakes

1 package (about 18 ounces) chocolate fudge cake mix *without* pudding in the mix
1 package (4-serving size) chocolate instant pudding and pie filling mix
1⅓ cups brewed coffee, cooled to room temperature
3 eggs
½ cup vegetable oil
1 teaspoon vanilla
½ gallon mocha or coffee ice cream, softened
1 bottle (7¼ ounces) quick-hardening chocolate shell dessert topping
½ cup pecan pieces, toasted*

*To toast pecans, spread in single layer on baking sheet. Bake in preheated 350°F oven 5 to 7 minutes or until fragrant, stirring frequently.

1. Preheat oven to 350°F. Line 20 standard (2½-inch) muffin cups with foil baking cups.

2. Beat cake mix, pudding mix, coffee, eggs, oil and vanilla in large bowl with electric mixer at low speed 30 seconds. Beat at medium speed 2 minutes or until well blended. Spoon evenly into prepared muffin cups.

3. Bake 20 minutes or until toothpick inserted into centers comes out clean. Cool in pans 10 minutes. Remove to wire racks; cool completely.

4. Remove 1 tablespoon cake from center of each cupcake. Fill each cupcake with 2 to 3 tablespoons ice cream, mounding slightly. Spoon about 1 tablespoon chocolate shell topping over ice cream; immediately sprinkle with pecans. Freeze until ready to serve. *Makes 20 cupcakes*

Spicy Coconut Lime Cupcakes

1¾ cups all-purpose flour
1½ teaspoons baking powder
 1 teaspoon salt
 ½ teaspoon baking soda
 ½ teaspoon ground red pepper
 ¾ cup granulated sugar
 ½ cup (1 stick) butter, softened
 ¾ cup canned coconut milk
 2 eggs
 ¼ cup milk
   Grated peel and juice of 2 limes
 ⅓ cup sweetened flaked coconut
   Coconut Lime Whipped Cream (page 83)
 ⅓ cup sweetened flaked coconut, toasted*
   Additional grated lime peel

*To toast coconut, spread evenly on ungreased baking sheet. Bake in 350°F oven
5 to 7 minutes or until light golden brown, stirring occasionally.*

1. Preheat oven to 350°F. Line 12 standard (2½-inch) muffin cups with paper baking cups.

2. Combine flour, baking powder, salt, baking soda and red pepper in medium bowl; mix well. Beat sugar and butter in large bowl with electric mixer at medium speed until creamy. Add coconut milk, eggs, milk, lime peel and lime juice; beat until well blended. Add flour mixture and ⅓ cup coconut; beat at low speed just until blended. Spoon evenly into prepared muffin cups.

3. Bake 18 to 20 minutes or until toothpick inserted into centers comes out clean. Cool in pan 5 minutes. Remove to wire rack; cool completely.

4. Prepare Coconut Lime Whipped Cream. Frost cupcakes; top with ⅓ cup toasted coconut and additional lime peel, if desired. Serve immediately or cover and refrigerate until ready to serve.   *Makes 12 cupcakes*

Coconut Lime Whipped Cream: Beat 1 cup whipping cream in large bowl with electric mixer at medium-high speed until soft peaks form. Add 2½ tablespoons coconut milk, 1 tablespoon sugar and grated peel and juice of 1 lime; beat until stiff peaks form.

Salted Caramel Cupcakes

1½ cups all-purpose flour
1 teaspoon baking powder
½ teaspoon salt
1 cup packed brown sugar
½ cup (1 stick) butter, softened
2 eggs
1 teaspoon vanilla
½ cup buttermilk
    Salted Caramel Frosting (recipe follows)
    Sea salt

1. Preheat oven to 325°F. Line 12 standard (2½-inch) muffin cups with paper baking cups.

2. Combine flour, baking powder and ½ teaspoon salt in small bowl; mix well. Beat brown sugar and butter in large bowl with electric mixer at medium speed until fluffy. Add eggs and vanilla; beat until well blended. Alternately add flour mixture and buttermilk, beating well after each addition. Spoon evenly into prepared muffin cups.

3. Bake 20 to 25 minutes or until toothpick inserted into centers comes out clean. Cool in pan 10 minutes. Remove to wire rack; cool completely.

4. Prepare Salted Caramel Frosting. Frost cupcakes; sprinkle with sea salt.

Makes 12 cupcakes

Salted Caramel Frosting: Combine ½ cup granulated sugar and 2 tablespoons water in large heavy saucepan; heat over high heat, without stirring, until medium amber in color. Remove from heat. Slowly stir in ¼ cup cream and 1 teaspoon sea salt (mixture will foam). Let stand 15 minutes. Beat 1 cup (2 sticks) softened butter and caramel mixture in large bowl with electric mixer at medium-high speed until well blended. Add 2½ cups powdered sugar; beat until thick and creamy. (If frosting is too soft, refrigerate 10 minutes before frosting cupcakes.)

Strawberry Milkshake Cupcakes

- 2 cups all-purpose flour
- 1½ cups granulated sugar
- 4 teaspoons baking powder
- ½ teaspoon salt
- 1¼ cups (2½ sticks) butter, softened, divided
- 1 cup plus 4 to 8 tablespoons milk, divided
- 2 teaspoons vanilla, divided
- 3 eggs
- 2 containers (7 ounces each) plain Greek yogurt
- 1 cup seedless strawberry preserves
- 6 cups powdered sugar, divided
- ¼ cup shortening
- Pink food coloring
- Assorted pastel sugar pearls and decorating sugar

1. Preheat oven to 350°F. Line 24 standard (2½-inch) muffin cups with paper baking cups.

2. Combine flour, granulated sugar, baking powder and salt in large bowl; mix well. Add ½ cup butter; beat with electric mixer at medium speed 30 seconds. Add 1 cup milk and 1 teaspoon vanilla; beat 2 minutes. Add eggs; beat 2 minutes. Spoon evenly into prepared muffin cups.

3. Bake 20 minutes or until toothpick inserted into centers comes out clean. Cool in pans 10 minutes. Remove to wire racks; cool completely.

4. Stir yogurt and preserves in medium bowl until well blended. Transfer to piping bag fitted with medium round tip. Insert tip into tops of cupcakes; squeeze bag gently to fill centers.

5. Beat 3 cups powdered sugar, remaining ¾ cup butter, shortening, 4 tablespoons milk and remaining 1 teaspoon vanilla in large bowl with electric mixer at low speed until smooth. Add remaining 3 cups powdered sugar; beat until light and fluffy. Add remaining milk, 1 tablespoon at a time, if necessary, to reach desired spreading consistency. Add food coloring, a few drops at a time, until desired shade is reached.

6. Frost cupcakes; decorate with sugar pearls and decorating sugar.

Makes 24 cupcakes

Maple Bacon Cupcakes

Cupcakes
- 1½ cups all-purpose flour
- 1¾ teaspoons baking powder
- ¾ cup granulated sugar
- ½ cup (1 stick) butter, softened
- 2 eggs
- 2 tablespoons maple syrup
- ½ cup milk
- 8 slices bacon, crisp-cooked and finely chopped, divided

Frosting
- ½ cup (1 stick) butter, softened
- 3 tablespoons maple syrup
- 2 tablespoons milk
- 3 cups powdered sugar

1. Preheat oven to 350°F. Line 12 standard (2½-inch) muffin cups with paper baking cups.

2. Combine flour and baking powder in small bowl; mix well. Beat granulated sugar and ½ cup butter in large bowl with electric mixer at medium speed until light and fluffy. Add eggs and 2 tablespoons maple syrup; beat until well blended. Add flour mixture and ½ cup milk; beat at low speed just until combined. Reserve 2 tablespoons bacon for topping; stir remaining bacon into batter. Spoon evenly into prepared muffin cups.

3. Bake 20 minutes or until toothpick inserted into centers comes out clean. Cool in pan 10 minutes. Remove to wire rack; cool completely.

4. Beat ½ cup butter, 3 tablespoons maple syrup and 2 tablespoons milk in large bowl with electric mixer at low speed 1 minute. Add powdered sugar; beat at medium speed until fluffy.

5. Frost cupcakes; top with reserved bacon.

Makes 12 cupcakes

Pineapple Zucchini Cupcakes
with Sour Cream Frosting

Cupcakes

> **1 package (about 18 ounces) yellow cake mix *without* pudding in the mix**
> **1 cup buttermilk**
> **3 eggs**
> **⅓ cup canola or vegetable oil**
> **1 teaspoon ground cinnamon**
> **½ teaspoon ground nutmeg**
> **¼ teaspoon ground allspice**
> **2 cups coarsely shredded zucchini (1 medium zucchini, unpeeled)**
> **1 can (8 ounces) crushed pineapple, well drained**

Frosting

> **4 cups powdered sugar**
> **⅔ cup sour cream**
> **¼ cup (½ stick) butter, softened**
> **2 teaspoons grated orange peel, plus additional for garnish**

1. Preheat oven to 350°F. Line 24 standard (2½-inch) muffin pan cups with paper baking cups; spray with nonstick cooking spray.

2. Beat cake mix, buttermilk, eggs, oil, cinnamon, nutmeg and allspice in large bowl with electric mixer at low speed 30 seconds or until moistened. Beat at medium speed 2 minutes. Stir in zucchini and pineapple; mix well. Spoon evenly into prepared muffin cups.

3. Bake 20 to 22 minutes or until toothpick inserted into centers comes out clean. Cool in pans 10 minutes. Remove to wire racks; cool completely.

4. Beat powdered sugar, sour cream and butter in large bowl with electric mixer at low speed. Beat at medium speed until smooth. Stir in 2 teaspoons orange peel.

5. Frost cupcakes; garnish with additional orange peel. Serve immediately or cover and refrigerate until ready to serve.   *Makes 24 cupcakes*

Cosmopolitan Cupcakes

   1 cup cranberry juice
  ¾ cup vodka
  ¼ cup orange juice
     Grated peel and juice of 2 limes
   1 package (about 18 ounces) white cake mix
  ⅓ cup vegetable oil
   2 eggs
   1 egg white
     Pink or red food coloring
  ½ cup (1 stick) butter, softened
   2 cups powdered sugar
     Coarse sugar

1. Preheat oven to 350°F. Line 24 standard (2½-inch) muffin cups with paper baking cups.

2. Combine cranberry juice, vodka, orange juice, lime peel and lime juice in large measuring cup; mix well.

3. Combine cake mix, 1 cup cranberry juice mixture, oil, eggs and egg white in large bowl; mix well. Add food coloring, one drop at a time, until desired shade is reached. Spoon evenly into prepared muffin cups.

4. Bake 20 minutes or until toothpick inserted into centers comes out clean. Brush tops of warm cupcakes with ½ cup cranberry mixture; cool completely in pans on wire racks.

5. Beat butter, powdered sugar and remaining ½ cup cranberry juice mixture in large bowl with electric mixer until fluffy. Add food coloring, one drop at a time, until desired shade is reached.

6. Frost cupcakes; sprinkle with coarse sugar. *Makes 24 cupcakes*

Seasonal Sensations

Apple Cider Cupcakes

- **1 package (about 18 ounces) spice cake mix**
- **1¼ cups apple cider**
- **3 eggs**
- **⅓ cup vegetable oil**
- **2 cups coarsely chopped walnuts, plus additional for garnish**
- **Apple Cider Frosting (recipe follows)**

1. Preheat oven to 350°F. Line 24 standard (2½-inch) muffin cups with paper baking cups.

2. Beat cake mix, apple cider, eggs and oil in medium bowl with electric mixer at low speed until blended. Beat at medium speed 2 minutes. Stir in 2 cups walnuts. Spoon evenly into prepared muffin cups.

3. Bake 20 minutes or until toothpick inserted into centers comes out clean. Cool in pans 10 minutes. Remove to wire racks; cool completely.

4. Prepare Apple Cider Frosting. Frost cupcakes; garnish with additional walnuts.

Makes 24 cupcakes

Apple Cider Frosting: Beat ½ cup (1 stick) softened butter and ¼ cup apple cider in medium bowl with electric mixer at low speed until well blended. Gradually beat in 4 cups powdered sugar until smooth.

Sweet Potato Spice Cupcakes

1¼ **pounds sweet potatoes, peeled and quartered**
1½ **cups all-purpose flour**
1¼ **cups granulated sugar**
  2 **teaspoons baking powder**
  1 **teaspoon ground cinnamon**
  ½ **teaspoon baking soda**
  ½ **teaspoon salt**
  ¼ **teaspoon ground allspice**
  ¾ **cup canola or vegetable oil**
  2 **eggs**
  ½ **cup chopped walnuts or pecans, plus additional for garnish**
  ½ **cup raisins**
     Cream Cheese Frosting (page 97)

1. Place sweet potatoes in large saucepan; add enough water to cover by 1 inch. Cover and cook over medium heat 30 minutes or until fork-tender, adding additional water, if necessary. Drain potatoes; mash when cool enough to handle. Measure 2 cups.

2. Preheat oven to 325°F. Line 18 standard (2½-inch) muffin cups with paper baking cups.

3. Combine flour, granulated sugar, baking powder, cinnamon, baking soda, salt and allspice in medium bowl; mix well. Beat sweet potatoes, oil and eggs in large bowl with electric mixer at low speed until blended. Add flour mixture; beat at medium speed 30 seconds or until blended. Stir in ½ cup walnuts and raisins. Spoon evenly into prepared muffin cups.

4. Bake 20 minutes or until toothpick inserted into centers comes out clean. Cool completely in pans on wire racks.

5. Prepare Cream Cheese Frosting. Frost cupcakes; sprinkle with additional walnuts. Serve immediately or cover and refrigerate until ready to serve.

Makes 18 cupcakes

Cream Cheese Frosting: Beat 1 package (8 ounces) softened cream cheese and ¼ cup (½ stick) softened butter in medium bowl with electric mixer at medium-high speed until creamy. Gradually beat in 1½ cups sifted powdered sugar until well blended. Beat in ¼ teaspoon salt and ¼ teaspoon vanilla.

Caramel Apple Cupcakes

**1 package (about 18 ounces) butter recipe yellow cake mix, plus ingredients
   to prepare mix**
1 cup chopped dried apples
   Caramel Frosting (recipe follows)
   Chopped pecans (optional)

1. Preheat oven to 375°F. Line 24 standard (2½-inch) muffin cups with paper baking cups.

2. Prepare cake mix according to package directions; stir in apples. Spoon batter evenly into prepared muffin cups.

3. Bake 20 minutes or until toothpick inserted into centers comes out clean. Cool in pans 10 minutes. Remove to wire racks; cool completely.

4. Prepare Caramel Frosting. Frost cupcakes; sprinkle with pecans.

Makes 24 cupcakes

Caramel Frosting

3 tablespoons butter
1 cup packed light brown sugar
½ cup evaporated milk
⅛ teaspoon salt
3¾ cups powdered sugar
¾ teaspoon vanilla

1. Melt butter in medium saucepan. Stir in brown sugar, evaporated milk and salt. Bring to a boil, stirring constantly. Remove to large bowl; cool slightly.

2. Add powdered sugar; beat with electric mixer at medium speed until smooth. Add vanilla; beat until frosting reaches desired spreading consistency.

Makes about 3 cups

Hot Chocolate Cupcakes

1 package (about 16 ounces) pound cake mix, plus ingredients to prepare mix
4 containers (4 ounces each) prepared chocolate pudding*
2½ cups whipped topping, divided
4 small chewy chocolate candies
Unsweetened cocoa powder

*Or prepare 1 package (4-serving size) instant chocolate pudding and pie filling mix according to package directions. Use 2 cups pudding for recipe; reserve remaining pudding for another use.

1. Preheat oven to 350°F. Spray 15 standard (2½-inch) muffin cups with baking spray (nonstick cooking spray with flour added) or grease and flour cups.

2. Prepare cake mix according to package directions. Spoon batter evenly into prepared muffin cups.

3. Bake 20 minutes or until toothpick inserted into centers comes out clean. Cool in pans 10 minutes. Remove to wire racks; cool completely.

4. Stir chocolate pudding and 2 cups whipped topping in medium bowl until well blended; cover and refrigerate until ready to use.

5. Working with one at a time, unwrap chocolate candies and microwave on LOW (30%) 5 to 10 seconds or until slightly softened. Stretch into long thin rope; cut into 2-inch lengths. Shape chocolate candy to resemble handles of mugs.

6. Cut two slits, ½ inch apart, in one side of each cupcake. Insert chocolate candy into slits.

7. Cut 2-inch hole from top of each cupcake with small paring knife. Fill with chocolate pudding mixture. Top evenly with remaining whipped topping; sprinkle with cocoa. *Makes 15 cupcakes*

Sweet Snowflakes

**1 package (about 18 ounces) white cake mix, plus ingredients
   to prepare mix**
4 ounces white chocolate candy discs
   White or blue sugar pearls and white nonpareils
1 container (16 ounces) white frosting

1. Preheat oven to 350°F. Line 24 standard (2½-inch) muffin cups with paper baking cups.

2. Prepare cake mix according to package directions. Spoon batter evenly into prepared muffin cups.

3. Bake 20 minutes or until toothpick inserted into centers comes out clean. Cool in pans 10 minutes. Remove to wire racks; cool completely.

4. Place large piece of waxed paper on work surface. Melt candy discs according to package directions; place in plastic squeeze bottle or piping bag fitted with small writing tip. Pipe snowflake shapes on waxed paper, a few at a time; immediately decorate with sugar pearls and nonpareils as desired. Repeat to create 24 large or 48 small snowflakes. Let stand 15 minutes or until set.

5. Frost cupcakes; top with snowflakes.

Makes 24 cupcakes

Festive Chocolate Cupcakes

¾ cup all-purpose flour
½ cup unsweetened cocoa powder
1 teaspoon baking powder
½ teaspoon salt
½ cup (1 stick) butter, softened
1 cup plus 2 tablespoons granulated sugar
2 eggs
1 teaspoon vanilla
½ cup whole milk
1½ cups prepared chocolate frosting
    Powdered sugar

1. Preheat oven to 350°F. Line 12 standard (2½-inch) muffin cups with paper baking cups.

2. Combine flour, cocoa, baking powder and salt in small bowl; mix well. Beat butter in large bowl with electric mixer at medium speed until creamy. Add granulated sugar; beat 3 to 4 minutes. Add eggs, one at a time, beating well after each addition. Beat in vanilla. Alternately add flour mixture and milk, beating well after each addition. Spoon evenly into prepared muffin cups.

3. Bake 20 minutes or until toothpick inserted into centers comes out clean. Cool in pan 10 minutes. Remove to wire rack; cool completely.

4. Microwave frosting in medium microwavable bowl on MEDIUM (50%) 30 seconds; stir. Microwave at additional 15-second intervals until frosting is melted. Dip tops of cupcakes in frosting; return to wire rack to set. (Frosting may need to be reheated several times to maintain melted consistency.)

5. When frosting is set, place stencil in desired shape on cupcake. Sprinkle with powdered sugar; carefully remove stencil.

Makes 12 cupcakes

Peppermint Mocha Cupcakes

1 package (about 18 ounces) dark chocolate cake mix, plus ingredients to prepare mix
1 tablespoon instant espresso powder
1½ cups whipping cream
1 package (12 ounces) semisweet chocolate chips
2 teaspoons peppermint extract
Crushed candy canes or peppermint candies

1. Preheat oven to 350°F. Line 24 standard (2½-inch) muffin cups with paper baking cups.

2. Prepare cake mix according to package directions; stir in espresso powder. Spoon batter evenly into prepared muffin cups.

3. Bake 20 minutes or until toothpick inserted into centers comes out clean. Cool in pans 10 minutes. Remove to wire racks; cool completely.

4. Bring cream to a simmer in small saucepan over medium heat. Place chocolate chips in medium heatproof bowl. Pour hot cream over chocolate chips; let stand 2 minutes. Whisk mixture until chocolate is melted and mixture is smooth. Stir in peppermint extract. Dip tops of cupcakes in chocolate mixture; return to wire racks. Let stand 10 minutes; dip tops again, if desired. Sprinkle with crushed candy canes.

Makes 24 cupcakes

Marshmallow Delights

     2 cups all-purpose flour
     1 teaspoon baking soda
     1 teaspoon baking powder
     ½ teaspoon salt
     ½ cup sour cream
     ½ cup milk
     1 teaspoon vanilla
     1 cup granulated sugar
     ½ cup (1 stick) butter, softened
     2 eggs
       Green food coloring
    1½ cups prepared white frosting
       Green decorating sugar (optional)
     3 cups fruit-flavored mini marshmallows

1. Preheat oven to 350°F. Line 12 standard (2½-inch) muffin cups with paper baking cups.

2. Combine flour, baking soda, baking powder and salt in medium bowl; mix well. Combine sour cream, milk and vanilla in small bowl; mix well. Beat granulated sugar and butter in large bowl with electric mixer at medium speed 2 minutes or until fluffy. Add eggs, one at a time, beating well after each addition. Alternately add flour mixture and sour cream mixture, beating well after each addition. Spoon evenly into prepared muffin cups.

3. Bake 20 minutes or until toothpick inserted into centers comes out clean. Cool in pan 10 minutes. Remove to wire rack; cool completely.

4. Add food coloring to frosting, a few drops at a time, until desired shade is reached. Frost cupcakes; sprinkle with decorating sugar, if desired. Arrange marshmallows over frosting.

Makes 12 cupcakes

Play Ball

    2 cups plus 1 tablespoon all-purpose flour, divided
    ¾ cup granulated sugar
    ¾ cup packed brown sugar
    1 tablespoon baking powder
    1 teaspoon salt
    ½ teaspoon baking soda
  1¼ cups milk
    3 eggs
    ½ cup shortening
  1½ teaspoons vanilla
    ½ cup mini semisweet chocolate chips
    1 container (16 ounces) vanilla frosting
      Food colorings, assorted candies and decors

1. Preheat oven to 350°F. Line 24 standard (2½-inch) muffin cups with paper baking cups.

2. Combine 2 cups flour, granulated sugar, brown sugar, baking powder, salt and baking soda in medium bowl; mix well. Beat milk, eggs, shortening and vanilla in large bowl with electric mixer at medium speed until well blended. Add flour mixture; beat at high speed 3 minutes, scraping side of bowl frequently. Toss chocolate chips with remaining 1 tablespoon flour in small bowl; stir into batter. Spoon evenly into prepared muffin cups.

3. Bake 20 minutes or until toothpick inserted into centers comes out clean. Cool in pans 10 minutes. Remove to wire racks; cool completely.

4. Decorate as desired to resemble baseballs, basketballs and/or other balls.

Makes 24 cupcakes

Raspberry Streusel Cupcakes

Streusel Topping (recipe follows)
3 cups all-purpose flour
2 teaspoons baking powder
½ teaspoon salt
⅛ teaspoon ground cinnamon
1½ cups sugar
½ cup (1 stick) butter, softened
2 eggs
1 teaspoon vanilla
1 cup sour cream
1½ pints fresh raspberries

1. Preheat oven to 350°F. Line 24 standard (2½-inch) muffin cups with paper baking cups. Prepare Streusel Topping.

2. Combine flour, baking powder, salt and cinnamon in medium bowl; mix well. Beat sugar and butter in large bowl with electric mixer at medium speed 2 to 3 minutes or until light and fluffy. Add eggs, one at a time, beating well after each addition. Stir in vanilla. Alternately add flour mixture and sour cream, beating well after each addition. Gently stir in raspberries. Spoon evenly into prepared muffin cups. Top evenly with Streusel Topping.

3. Bake 20 to 25 minutes or until toothpick inserted into centers comes out clean. Cool in pans 10 minutes. Remove to wire racks; cool completely.

Makes 24 cupcakes

Streusel Topping: Combine 1 cup sugar, ⅔ cup all-purpose flour, ¼ cup pecan chips, 1 teaspoon ground cinnamon and ¼ teaspoon salt in medium bowl. Cut ½ cup (1 stick) butter into small pieces; cut butter and 1 tablespoon milk into sugar mixture with pastry blender or two knives until mixture resembles coarse crumbs.

Blueberry Buttermilk Cupcakes

¾ cup fresh blueberries, plus additional for garnish
1¾ cups all-purpose flour
2 teaspoons baking powder
½ teaspoon salt
¼ teaspoon baking soda
½ cup granulated sugar
¼ cup (½ stick) butter, softened
1 egg
Grated peel of 1 lemon
1 tablespoon plus 1 teaspoon lemon juice, divided
1 cup plus 2 tablespoons buttermilk, divided
1½ to 2 cups powdered sugar

1. Freeze ¾ cup blueberries 30 minutes.

2. Preheat oven to 350°F. Line 12 standard (2½-inch) muffin cups with paper baking cups. Place frozen blueberries in food processor; process until finely chopped.

3. Combine flour, baking powder, salt and baking soda in small bowl; mix well. Beat granulated sugar and butter in large bowl with electric mixer at medium speed until creamy. Add egg, lemon peel and 1 tablespoon lemon juice; beat until blended. Add flour mixture, 1 cup buttermilk and chopped blueberries; beat at low speed just until combined. Spoon evenly into prepared muffin cups.

4. Bake 20 minutes or until toothpick inserted into centers comes out clean. Cool in pan 5 minutes. Remove to wire rack; cool completely.

5. Whisk remaining 2 tablespoons buttermilk, 1 teaspoon lemon juice and 1½ cups powdered sugar in medium bowl until smooth. Add additional powdered sugar, if necessary, until desired spreading consistency is reached.

6. Dip tops of cupcakes into icing to coat; return to wire rack. Garnish with additional blueberries; drizzle with remaining icing. *Makes 12 cupcakes*

Pink Lemonade Cupcakes

1 package (about 18 ounces) white cake mix *without* pudding in the mix
1 cup water
3 egg whites
⅓ cup plus ¼ cup frozen pink lemonade concentrate, divided
2 tablespoons vegetable oil
5 to 8 drops red food coloring, divided
4 cups powdered sugar
⅓ cup butter, softened
Lemon slice candies (optional)

1. Preheat oven to 350°F. Line 24 standard (2½-inch) muffin cups with paper baking cups.

2. Beat cake mix, water, egg whites, ⅓ cup lemonade concentrate, oil and 4 to 6 drops food coloring in large bowl with electric mixer at medium speed 2 minutes or until well blended. Spoon evenly into prepared muffin cups.

3. Bake 20 minutes or until toothpick inserted into centers comes out clean. Cool in pans 10 minutes. Remove to wire racks; cool completely.

4. Beat powdered sugar, butter and remaining ¼ cup lemonade concentrate in medium bowl with electric mixer at medium speed until well blended. Beat in remaining 1 to 2 drops food coloring until desired shade is reached.

5. Frost cupcakes; garnish with candies. *Makes 24 cupcakes*

Tip: To make these colorful cupcakes look even more like glasses of refreshing pink lemonade, you can trim bendable plastic straws to fit and press them into the top of the cupcakes.

Peaches & Cream Cupcakes

1 cup all-purpose flour
¼ cup cornmeal
1 teaspoon baking powder
½ teaspoon baking soda
½ teaspoon salt
¾ cup granulated sugar
½ cup (1 stick) butter, softened
2 eggs
1½ teaspoons vanilla, divided
⅓ cup buttermilk
1 large ripe peach, peeled and finely chopped (about 1 cup)
½ cup peach jam
1 cup whipping cream
1 tablespoon powdered sugar
1 medium ripe peach, diced

1. Preheat oven to 350°F. Line 12 standard (2½-inch) muffin cups with paper baking cups.

2. Combine flour, cornmeal, baking powder, baking soda and salt in medium bowl; mix well. Beat granulated sugar and butter in large bowl with electric mixer at medium speed until creamy. Add eggs and 1 teaspoon vanilla; beat until well blended. Add flour mixture; beat at low speed while adding buttermilk just until combined. Stir in finely chopped peach. Spoon evenly into prepared muffin cups.

3. Bake 20 to 22 minutes or until toothpick inserted into centers comes out clean. Cool in pan 5 minutes. Remove to wire rack; cool completely.

4. Cut 1-inch holes in top of each cupcake, reserving cupcake pieces. Fill each hole with 2 teaspoons peach jam; replace tops.

5. Beat cream in large bowl with electric mixer at medium-high speed until soft peaks form. Add powdered sugar and remaining ½ teaspoon vanilla; beat until stiff peaks form. Top cupcakes with whipped cream; garnish with diced peach.

Makes 12 cupcakes

Sweet Surprises

Peanut Butter & Jelly Cupcakes

1 package (about 18 ounces) yellow cake mix, plus ingredients
    to prepare mix
2 cups strawberry jelly
¾ cup creamy peanut butter
½ cup (1 stick) butter, softened
2 cups powdered sugar
½ teaspoon vanilla
¼ cup milk

1. Preheat oven to 350°F. Line 22 standard (2½-inch) muffin cups with paper baking cups.

2. Prepare cake mix according to package directions. Spoon batter evenly into prepared muffin cups. Bake 20 minutes or until toothpick inserted into centers comes out clean. Cool in pans 10 minutes. Remove to wire racks; cool completely.

3. Place jelly in pastry bag fitted with small round tip. Insert tip into tops of cupcakes; squeeze bag gently to fill centers with jelly.

4. Beat peanut butter and butter in medium bowl with electric mixer at medium speed 2 minutes or until smooth. Add powdered sugar and vanilla; beat at low speed 1 minute or until crumbly. Slowly add milk, beating until creamy. Frost cupcakes.

Makes 22 cupcakes

Boston Cream Cupcakes

1 package (about 18 ounces) yellow cake mix, plus ingredients to prepare mix

1 cup milk

¼ cup French vanilla instant pudding and pie filling mix

1 container (16 ounces) dark chocolate frosting

1. Preheat oven to 350°F. Spray 22 standard (2½-inch) muffin cups with nonstick cooking spray.

2. Prepare cake mix according to package directions. Spoon batter evenly into prepared muffin cups.

3. Bake 15 to 20 minutes or until toothpick inserted into centers comes out clean. Cool in pans 10 minutes. Remove to wire racks; cool completely.

4. Meanwhile, whisk milk and pudding mix in medium bowl 2 minutes. Cover and refrigerate until set.

5. Gently poke small hole into bottom of each cupcake with tip of knife. Spoon pudding into pastry bag fitted with small round tip. Insert tip into tops of cupcakes; squeeze bag gently to fill cupcakes with pudding.

6. Microwave frosting in medium microwavable bowl on HIGH 30 seconds; stir. Frost cupcakes.

Makes 22 cupcakes

Decadent Brownie Cupcakes

1 cup (2 sticks) butter
4 squares (4 ounces) squares unsweetened chocolate
2 cups sugar
4 eggs
1 teaspoon vanilla
1 cup all-purpose flour
½ teaspoon salt
20 mini chocolate peanut butter cups

1. Preheat oven to 350°F. Line 20 standard (2½-inch) muffin cups with foil baking cups.

2. Heat butter and chocolate in large saucepan over very low heat until melted and smooth, stirring frequently. Remove from heat.

3. Gradually stir sugar into chocolate mixture until well blended. Add eggs, one at a time, beating well after each addition. Stir in vanilla. Combine flour and salt; stir into chocolate mixture until well blended. Spoon evenly into prepared muffin cups. Place 1 peanut butter cup in center of each cup.

4. Bake 18 minutes or until toothpick inserted near centers comes out clean. Serve warm or remove to wire racks; cool completely.   *Makes 20 cupcakes*

Double Raspberry Cream Filled Cupcakes

Cupcakes
- 1 package white cake mix

Raspberry Filling
- 1 package (8 ounces) cream cheese, softened
- 1 egg
- 3 tablespoons fresh or frozen (thawed) raspberries
- ⅓ cup granulated sugar
- 1 teaspoon SPICE ISLANDS® 100% Pure Bourbon Vanilla Extract

Raspberry Frosting
- 3 cups powdered sugar
- ¼ cup (½ stick) butter or margarine, softened
- 2 tablespoons fresh or frozen (thawed) raspberries
- 1 teaspoon SPICE ISLANDS® 100% Pure Bourbon Vanilla Extract
- 1 to 3 tablespoons milk

PREPARE cake mix according to package directions. Combine all filling ingredients in medium bowl and beat with mixer. Grease and flour muffin pans or line with paper liners.

FILL cups ⅓ full with cake batter. Add 1½ to 2 teaspoons Raspberry Filling to the center of each cupcake, then top with enough cake batter to fill cups ½ full.

BAKE in a 350°F preheated oven 20 to 25 minutes, or until toothpick inserted into centers comes out clean. Let cool 10 minutes in pan; finish cooling on wire rack.

COMBINE all frosting ingredients except milk in medium bowl. Beat with electric mixer, gradually adding enough milk to reach desired consistency.

FROST cupcakes when cool; refrigerate cupcakes until ready to serve.

Makes 30 cupcakes

Prep Time: 30 minutes • **Bake Time:** 20 to 25 minutes • **Cool Time:** 30 minutes

Banana Cream Pie Cupcakes

**1 package (about 18 ounces) yellow cake mix, plus ingredients
    to prepare mix**
2 cups milk
1 package (4-serving size) banana instant pudding and pie filling mix
2 bananas
2 tablespoons sugar, divided
2 cups whipping cream

1. Preheat oven to 350°F. Line 24 standard (2½-inch) muffin cups with paper baking cups.

2. Prepare cake mix according to package directions. Spoon batter evenly into prepared muffin cups.

3. Bake 20 minutes or until toothpick inserted into centers comes out clean. Cool in pans 10 minutes. Remove to wire racks; cool completely.

4. Meanwhile, whisk milk and pudding mix in medium bowl 2 minutes. Cover and refrigerate until set.

5. Preheat broiler. Line baking sheet with parchment paper. Cut each banana into 12 slices. Place 1 tablespoon sugar in shallow bowl. Dip one side each of banana slice in sugar; place on prepared baking sheet, sugar side up. Broil 2 minutes or until golden brown. Cool completely.

6. Beat cream and remaining 1 tablespoon sugar in large bowl with electric mixer at medium-high speed until stiff peaks form.

7. Cut 1-inch hole in tops of cupcakes; discard cupcake pieces. Fill holes with pudding (reserve remaining pudding for another use). Place whipped cream in piping bag fitted with large star tip; pipe whipped cream over filling. Top each cupcake with 1 banana slice. *Makes 24 cupcakes*

Surprise Prize Cupcakes

1 package (18.25 ounces) plain chocolate cake mix
⅓ cup water
3 large eggs
⅓ cup vegetable oil
1 package (16.5 ounces) NESTLÉ® TOLL HOUSE® Refrigerated Chocolate Chip Cookie Bar Dough
1 container (16 ounces) prepared chocolate frosting
NESTLÉ® TOLL HOUSE® Semi-Sweet Chocolate Mini Morsels

PREHEAT oven to 350°F. Paper-line 24 muffin cups.

BEAT cake mix, water, eggs and oil in large mixer bowl on low speed for 30 seconds. Beat on medium speed for 2 minutes or until smooth. Spoon about ¼ cup batter into each cup, filling about two-thirds full.

CUT cookie dough into 24 pieces; roll each into a ball. Place one ball of dough in each muffin cup, pressing it into the bottom.

BAKE for 19 to 22 minutes or until top springs back when gently touched. Let stand for 15 minutes. Remove to wire rack to cool completely. Spread with frosting and sprinkle with morsels. *Makes 2 dozen cupcakes*

Prep Time: 15 minutes • **Baking Time:** 19 minutes • **Cooling Time:** 30 minutes

Hidden Berry Cupcakes

1¾ cups all-purpose flour
1¼ cups granulated sugar
  1 tablespoon baking powder
  ½ teaspoon salt
  ⅓ cup (5 tablespoons plus 1 teaspoon) butter, softened
  3 eggs
  ⅔ cup milk
  1 tablespoon vanilla
  1 cup QUAKER® Oats (quick or old fashioned, uncooked)
  ½ cup seedless strawberry or raspberry fruit spread
     Confectioners' sugar

1. Heat oven to 350°F. Line 16 medium muffin cups with paper or foil liners. Set aside.

2. Combine flour, sugar, baking powder and salt in large bowl. Add butter and beat with electric mixer on low speed until crumbly, about 1 minute. Combine eggs, milk and vanilla in medium bowl; add to flour mixture. Beat on low speed until incorporated, then on medium speed 2 minutes. Gently fold in oats. Divide batter evenly among muffin cups, filling each about ¾ full.

3. Bake 18 minutes or until a wooden pick inserted in center comes out clean. Remove from pan; cool completely on wire rack.

4. Using small sharp knife, cut cone-shaped piece from center of each cupcake, leaving ¾-inch border around edge of cupcake. Carefully remove and reserve cake pieces. Fill each depression with generous teaspoon of fruit spread. Top with reserved cake pieces; sift confectioners' sugar over tops of cupcakes.

Makes 16 cupcakes

Chocolate Espresso Surprises

Ganache Frosting (*page 135*)
½ cup unsweetened cocoa powder
1 tablespoon espresso or instant coffee granules
⅔ cup boiling water
4 squares (4 ounces) bittersweet chocolate, finely chopped
2 cups all-purpose flour
1 teaspoon baking soda
¼ teaspoon salt
1½ cups sugar
¾ cup (1½ sticks) butter, softened
4 eggs
2 teaspoons vanilla
1 cup sour cream

1. Prepare Ganache Frosting.

2. Preheat oven to 350°F. Line 24 (2½-inch) muffin cups with paper baking cups.

3. Combine cocoa and espresso powder in small bowl. Whisk in boiling water until cocoa is dissolved. Add chocolate; whisk until melted. Combine flour, baking soda and salt in medium bowl; mix well. Beat sugar and butter in large bowl with electric mixer at medium speed until light and fluffy. Add eggs, one at a time, beating well after each addition. Stir in vanilla and chocolate mixture until combined. Alternately add flour mixture and sour cream, beating at low speed after each addition until just combined. Spoon evenly into prepared muffin cups.

4. Bake 17 to 20 minutes or until toothpick inserted into centers comes out clean. Cool in pans 3 to 5 minutes. Remove to wire racks; cool completely.

5. Place frosting in pastry bag fitted with small star tip. Insert tip into tops of cupcakes; squeeze gently to fill centers with frosting. Pipe stars on top. *Makes 24 cupcakes*

Ganache Frosting

1½ cups whipping cream
12 squares (12 ounces) bittersweet chocolate, chopped
2 tablespoons (¼ stick) butter, cut into small pieces
3 tablespoons coffee liqueur
1½ teaspoons vanilla

1. Bring cream and butter to a simmer in small saucepan over medium-high heat, stirring occasionally.

2. Place chocolate in food processor. With processor running, slowly add hot cream mixture through feed tube; process 4 minutes or until smooth and thickened. Stir in coffee liqueur and vanilla. Transfer to small bowl; cover and let stand 3 to 4 hours or until desired spreading consistency is reached. ***Makes about 3 cups***

Carrot Cream Cheese Cupcakes

   1 package (8 ounces) cream cheese, softened
¼ cup powdered sugar
   1 package (about 18 ounces) spice cake mix, plus ingredients
      to prepare mix
   2 cups grated carrots
   2 tablespoons finely chopped crystallized ginger*
   1 container (16 ounces) cream cheese frosting
   3 tablespoons maple syrup
     Orange peel strips (optional)

Crystallized ginger is available in some large supermarkets in the spice aisle and in Asian markets.

1. Preheat oven to 350°F. Spray 14 jumbo (3½-inch) muffin cups with nonstick cooking spray or line with paper baking cups.

2. Beat cream cheese and powdered sugar in large bowl with electric mixer at medium speed 1 minute or until light and fluffy.

3. Prepare cake mix according to package directions; stir in carrots and ginger. Spoon batter evenly into prepared muffin cups. Place 1 tablespoon cream cheese mixture in center of each cup. Top evenly with remaining batter.

4. Bake 25 to 28 minutes or until toothpick inserted into centers comes out clean. Cool in pans 10 minutes. Remove to wire racks; cool completely.

5. Stir frosting and maple syrup in medium bowl until well blended.

6. Frost cupcakes; garnish with orange peel.　　　　*Makes 14 jumbo cupcakes*

Fudge 'n' Banana Cupcakes

　　1 package **DUNCAN HINES® Moist Deluxe® Devil's Food Cake Mix**
　　3 **large eggs**
　1⅓ **cups water**
　　½ **cup vegetable oil**
　　½ **cup (1 stick) butter or margarine**
　　2 **squares (2 ounces) unsweetened chocolate**
　　1 **pound confectioners' sugar**
　　½ **cup half-and-half**
　　1 **teaspoon vanilla extract**
　　4 **medium bananas**
　　2 **tablespoons lemon juice**

1. Preheat oven to 350°F. Place paper liners into 24 standard (2½-inch) muffin cups. Combine cake mix, eggs, water and oil in large bowl. Prepare, bake and cool cupcakes as directed on package.

2. For frosting,* melt butter and chocolate in heavy saucepan over low heat. Remove from heat. Add confectioners' sugar alternately with half-and-half, mixing until smooth after each addition. Beat in vanilla extract. Add more confectioners' sugar to thicken or half-and-half to thin as needed.

3. Using small paring knife, remove cone-shaped piece from top center of each cupcake. Dot top of each cone with frosting. Frost top of each cupcake spreading frosting down into cone-shaped hole. Slice bananas and dip in lemon juice. Stand three banana slices in each hole. Set cone-shaped pieces, pointed side down, on banana slices.
　　　　　　　　　　　　　　　　　　　　　　　　Makes 24 cupcakes

Or use 1 can DUNCAN HINES® Chocolate Frosting.

Drizzled Surprise Cupcakes

  1 package (about 18 ounces) yellow cake mix
  1 cup milk
  3 eggs
  ⅓ cup vegetable oil
  ½ cup creamy peanut butter
  1 teaspoon vanilla
 34 dark chocolate bite-size candies, unwrapped, divided

1. Preheat oven to 350°F. Line 24 standard (2½-inch) muffin cups with paper baking cups.

2. Beat cake mix, milk, eggs and oil in large bowl with electric mixer at low speed 30 seconds or until moistened. Beat at medium speed 2 minutes. Add peanut butter and vanilla; beat just until blended. Spoon 2 tablespoons batter into each muffin cup; top with 1 chocolate candy. Spoon remaining batter evenly into muffin cups, covering each candy completely with batter.

3. Bake 18 to 20 minutes or until lightly browned and centers spring back when lightly touched. Cool in pans 15 minutes. Remove to wire racks; cool completely.

4. Heat remaining 10 chocolate candies in small microwavable bowl on HIGH 30 seconds. Stir; heat at 10-second intervals until chocolate is melted and smooth. Drizzle evenly over cupcakes; let stand until set. *Makes 24 cupcakes*

Pumpkin Pie Surprise Cupcakes

1 package (18 ounces) yellow cake mix, plus ingredients
    to prepare mix
1 teaspoon ground cinnamon
1 (9-inch) refrigerated pie crust
3 cups whipping cream
1½ cups canned pumpkin pie filling
    Ground nutmeg

1. Preheat oven to 350°F. Line 20 standard (2½-inch) muffin cups with paper baking cups.

2. Prepare cake mix according to package directions; stir in cinnamon. Spoon batter evenly into prepared muffin cups. Bake 20 minutes or until toothpick inserted into centers comes out clean. Cool completely in pans on wire racks.

3. Meanwhile, prepare pumpkin cutouts. *Increase oven temperature to 400°F.* Line baking sheet with parchment paper. Unroll pie crust onto work surface. Using cookie cutter or sharp paring knife, cut out 20 small (1- to 2-inch) pumpkins. Place on baking sheet; score vertical lines in each pumpkin to resemble ridges. Bake 10 minutes or until light golden brown. Remove to wire racks; cool completely.

4. Beat cream in large bowl with electric mixer at medium-high speed until stiff peaks form. Combine 1 cup whipped cream and pumpkin pie filling in medium bowl; mix well.

5. Cut hole in center of each cupcake; discard cupcake pieces. Using spoon or piping bag fitted with round tip, fill each hole with about 1 tablespoon filling. Top evenly with remaining whipped cream; sprinkle lightly with nutmeg. Garnish with pumpkin cutouts.   *Makes 20 cupcakes*

Holiday Delights

Chocolate Sweetheart Cupcakes

**1 package (about 18 ounces) chocolate cake mix, plus ingredients
to prepare mix**
1 container (16 ounces) vanilla frosting
3 tablespoons seedless raspberry jam

1. Preheat oven to 350°F. Line 24 standard (2½-inch) muffin cups with paper baking cups.

2. Prepare cake mix according to package directions. Spoon batter evenly into prepared muffin cups.

3. Bake 20 minutes or until toothpick inserted into centers comes out clean. Cool in pans 10 minutes. Remove to wire racks; cool completely.

4. Cut off rounded tops of cupcakes with serrated knife. Cut out heart shape from each cupcake top with mini cookie cutter; reserve cutouts, if desired.

5. Stir frosting and jam in medium bowl until well blended. Spread frosting mixture generously over cupcake bottoms, mounding slightly in center. Replace cupcake tops, pressing gently to fill hearts with frosting mixture. Garnish with heart cutouts, if desired. *Makes 24 cupcakes*

Sweetheart Strawberry Cupcakes

1 cup coarsely chopped strawberries, divided
1½ cups all-purpose flour
1 teaspoon baking powder
½ teaspoon baking soda
½ teaspoon salt
¾ cup granulated sugar
½ cup (1 stick) butter, softened
2 eggs
1 teaspoon vanilla
⅓ cup buttermilk
Tangy Strawberry Buttercream (page 147)
6 small strawberries, halved

1. Preheat oven to 350°F. Line 12 standard (2½-inch) muffin cups with paper baking cups.

2. Place ¾ cup chopped strawberries in food processor; process until smooth. Reserve 2 tablespoons for frosting.

3. Combine flour, baking powder, baking soda and salt in medium bowl; mix well. Beat granulated sugar and butter in large bowl with electric mixer at medium speed until creamy. Add ½ cup strawberry purée until blended. Add eggs and vanilla; beat until well blended. Add flour mixture; beat at low speed while adding buttermilk just until combined. Stir in remaining ¼ cup chopped strawberries. Spoon evenly into prepared muffin cups.

4. Bake 20 to 22 minutes or until toothpick inserted into centers comes out clean. Cool in pan 5 minutes. Remove to wire rack; cool completely.

5. Prepare Tangy Strawberry Buttercream. Frost cupcakes. Cut strawberry halves to resemble hearts; top each cupcake with strawberry heart.   *Makes 12 cupcakes*

Tangy Strawberry Buttercream

½ cup (1 stick) butter, softened
4 ounces cream cheese, softened
2 tablespoons reserved strawberry purée
2 to 2½ cups powdered sugar

Beat butter, cream cheese and strawberry purée in large bowl with electric mixer at medium speed until well blended. Gradually add powdered sugar, beating until desired spreading consistency is reached.
Makes about 1cup

Magically Minty Mini Cupcakes

**1 package (about 18 ounces) chocolate cake mix, plus ingredients
to prepare mix**
2 teaspoons mint extract
1 container (16 ounces) white frosting
**Green and white sprinkles, green decorating sugar or shamrock
candy decors**

1. Preheat oven to 350°F. Line 60 mini (1¾-inch) muffin cups with paper baking cups.

2. Prepare cake mix according to package directions; stir in mint extract. Spoon batter evenly into prepared muffin cups.

3. Bake 10 minutes or until toothpick inserted into centers comes out clean. Cool in pans 5 minutes. Remove to wire racks; cool completely.

4. Frost cupcakes; top with sprinkles, decorating sugar or candy decors.

Makes 60 mini cupcakes

Easter Chicks

**1 package (about 18 ounces) yellow cake mix, plus ingredients
   to prepare mix**
2 containers (16 ounces each) white frosting
   Pink and yellow food coloring
   Orange chewy fruit candy squares
   Black decorating gel

1. Preheat oven to 350°F. Line 60 mini (1¾-inch) muffin cups with paper baking cups.

2. Prepare cake mix according to package directions. Spoon batter evenly into prepared muffin cups.

3. Bake 10 minutes or until toothpick inserted into centers comes out clean. Cool in pans 5 minutes. Remove to wire racks; cool completely.

4. Using serrated knife, cut off rounded domes of cupcakes so tops are flat. Remove baking cups from half of cupcakes.

5. Divide frosting between two small bowls. Add food coloring, a few drops at a time, until desired shades are reached. Spread small amount of frosting evenly in center of cupcakes with baking cups. Place cupcakes without baking cups upside down over frosting; press gently to seal cupcakes together.

6. Frost cupcakes, mounding extra frosting on top to create egg shape.

7. Working with one at a time, unwrap candy squares and microwave on LOW (30%) 5 to 10 seconds or until softened. Press candy between hands or on waxed paper to flatten to ⅛-inch thickness. Using scissors or paring knife, cut out triangles for beaks. Create faces on chicks with candy beaks and dots of decorating gel for eyes.

Makes 30 cupcakes

All-American Cupcakes

1 package (about 18 ounces) cake mix, any flavor, plus ingredients to prepare mix
1 container (16 ounces) white frosting
Blue candy stars
Red string licorice

1. Preheat oven to 350°F. Line 22 standard (2½-inch) muffin cups with paper baking cups.

2. Prepare cake mix according to package directions. Spoon batter evenly into prepared muffin cups.

3. Bake 20 minutes or until toothpick inserted into centers comes out clean. Cool in pans 10 minutes. Remove to wire racks; cool completely.

4. Frost cupcakes; arrange candy stars in left corner of each cupcake. Arrange licorice in rows across remaining portion of each cupcake, cutting pieces to fit.

Makes 22 cupcakes

Tip: Blue candy stars can be found in the bulk section of candy stores and at some craft stores. If you can't find them, you can substitute mini candy-coated chocolate pieces or blue candy dots.

Mini Fireworks

**1 package (about 18 ounces) chocolate cake mix, plus ingredients
to prepare mix**
4 ounces white chocolate candy discs
  Red, white and blue decorating sugar
1 container (16 ounces) chocolate frosting

1. Preheat oven to 350°F. Line 60 mini (1¾-inch) muffin cups with paper baking cups.

2. Prepare cake mix according to package directions. Spoon batter evenly into prepared muffin cups.

3. Bake 10 minutes or until toothpick inserted into centers comes out clean. Cool in pans 5 minutes. Remove to wire racks; cool completely.

4. Place large piece of waxed paper on work surface. Melt candy discs according to package directions; place in plastic squeeze bottle or piping bag fitted with small round tip. Pipe firework shapes on waxed paper, a few at a time; immediately sprinkle with decorating sugar. Repeat to create 60 large or 120 small fireworks. Let stand 15 minutes or until set.

5. Frost cupcakes; top with fireworks.

Makes 60 mini cupcakes

Friendly Ghost Cupcakes

1⅓ cups all-purpose flour
¾ cup unsweetened cocoa powder
2 teaspoons baking powder
½ teaspoon salt
¼ teaspoon baking soda
1 cup sugar
6 tablespoons (¾ stick) butter, softened
2 eggs
1 teaspoon vanilla
¾ cup milk
1 cup prepared chocolate frosting
4 cups whipped topping
Mini semisweet chocolate chips

1. Preheat oven to 350°F. Line 14 standard (2½-inch) muffin cups with paper baking cups.

2. Combine flour, cocoa, baking powder, salt and baking soda in medium bowl; mix well. Beat sugar and butter in large bowl with electric mixer at medium speed until fluffy. Add eggs and vanilla; beat until well blended. Add flour mixture and milk; beat at low speed just until combined. Spoon evenly into prepared muffin cups.

3. Bake 15 minutes or until toothpick inserted into centers comes out clean. Cool in pans 10 minutes. Remove to wire racks; cool completely.

4. Place frosting in medium microwavable bowl. Microwave on HIGH 10 seconds or until slightly melted. Dip tops of cupcakes in frosting; return to wire racks. Let stand until set.

5. Place whipped topping in piping bag fitted with large round tip or resealable food storage bag with 1 inch cut off one corner of bag. Pipe ghost shape onto each cupcake. Add chocolate chips for eyes. Serve immediately or cover and refrigerate until ready to serve.   *Makes 14 cupcakes*

Spider Web Pull-Apart Cake

**1 package (9 ounces) yellow cake mix, plus ingredients
    to prepare mix**
Red and yellow food coloring
1 container (16 ounces) white frosting
Black decorating icing
1 black licorice
1 small chocolate wafer
2 mini marshmallows

1. Preheat oven to 350°F. Line 12 standard (2½-inch) muffin cups with paper baking cups.

2. Prepare cake mix according to package directions. Spoon batter evenly into prepared muffin cups.

3. Bake 20 minutes or until toothpick inserted into centers comes out clean. Cool in pan 10 minutes. Remove to wire rack; cool completely.

4. Place 1 cupcake in center of serving platter; arrange remaining 6 cupcakes around center. Reserve remaining 5 cupcakes for another use.

5. Add food coloring to frosting, a few drops at a time, until desired shade is reached. Frost cupcakes, spreading frosting so that entire top is covered (as shown in photo).

6. Starting in center, pipe decorating icing in spiral pattern. Using toothpick or small knife, draw lines from center to outer edge of cupcakes to create web pattern.

7. Cut licorice into eight pieces; place in two rows of four on one end of web for spider legs. Top with wafer. Dot icing on bottom of each marshmallow; place on wafer. Pipe small dot of icing on each marshmallow for eyes.   *Makes 7 servings*

Feathered Friends

**1 package (19 to 21 ounces) brownie mix, plus ingredients
to prepare mix**
Red, orange and yellow gummy fish candies
1½ containers (16 ounces each) chocolate frosting
White decorating icing
Mini semisweet chocolate chips

1. Preheat oven to 350°F. Line 12 standard (2½-inch) muffin cups with paper baking cups.

2. Prepare brownie mix according to package directions for cakelike brownies. Spoon batter evenly into prepared muffin cups.

3. Bake 24 minutes or until toothpick inserted into centers comes out clean. Cool in pan 10 minutes. Remove to wire rack; cool completely.

4. Using sharp knife, cut gummy fish in half lengthwise to create two thinner fish. Cut tails off of each fish; reserve tails.

5. Frost cupcakes. Arrange 12 gummy fish halves, cut sides facing you, in two rows on one side of each cupcake, pressing cut ends of fish into cupcake (as shown in photo).

6. Place remaining frosting in pastry bag fitted with large round tip or resealable food storage bag with 1-inch corner cut off. Pipe 1½-inch mound of frosting on opposite side of each cupcake to create head. Pipe eyes with decorating icing; place mini chocolate chip in center of each eye. Use reserved gummy fish tails to create beaks. *Makes 12 cupcakes*

Double Gingerbread Cupcakes

1¾ cups all-purpose flour
 1 teaspoon ground cinnamon
 1 teaspoon ground ginger
 ¾ teaspoon salt, divided
 ½ teaspoon baking soda
 ½ teaspoon ground allspice
 ¾ cup (1½ sticks) butter, softened, divided
 ½ cup packed brown sugar
 1 egg
 3 tablespoons molasses
 1 package (14½ ounces) gingerbread cake and cookie mix,*
   plus ingredients to prepare mix
   White decorating icing and red decors (optional)
 1 package (8 ounces) cream cheese, softened
 2 cups powdered sugar

If gingerbread cake mix is not available, substitute spice cake mix; add 2 teaspoons ground ginger to batter. Spice cake mix will make 22 to 24 cupcakes; use 12 for this recipe and reserve remaining cupcakes for another use.

1. Combine flour, cinnamon, ginger, ½ teaspoon salt, baking soda and allspice in medium bowl; mix well. Beat ½ cup butter and brown sugar in large bowl with electric mixer at medium speed 5 minutes or until light and fluffy. Add egg and molasses; beat until well blended. Add flour mixture; beat at low speed until well blended. Divide dough in half; wrap and refrigerate at least 2 hours or up to 24 hours.**

2. Preheat oven to 350°F. Line 12 standard (2½-inch) muffin cups with paper baking cups.

3. Prepare gingerbread mix according to package directions for cake. Spoon batter evenly into prepared muffin cups.

4. Bake 20 minutes or until toothpick inserted into centers comes out clean. Cool in pan 10 minutes. Remove to wire rack; cool completely.

5. Line cookie sheets with parchment paper. Roll out half of dough to ⅛-inch thickness on lightly floured surface. Cut out shapes with 1½-inch gingerbread man cookie cutter. Place cutouts 1 inch apart on prepared cookie sheets.

6. Bake 5 minutes or until edges are lightly browned. Cool on cookie sheets 1 minute. Remove to wire racks; cool completely.

7. Decorate cookies with decorating icing and decors, if desired.

8. Beat cream cheese, remaining ¼ cup butter and ¼ teaspoon salt in medium bowl with electric mixer at medium-high speed until creamy. Gradually beat in powdered sugar until well blended.

9. Frost cupcakes; top with cookies.   *Makes 12 cupcakes*

**Only half of dough is needed for the cupcake toppers. The remaining cookie dough may be refrigerated or frozen for later use.

Cupcake Ornaments

1 package (about 18 ounces) yellow cake mix, plus ingredients to prepare mix
1 container (16 ounces) vanilla frosting
Decorating sugar (optional)
Red string licorice
Green and red fruit roll-ups
Small shaped candies
22 gumdrops

1. Preheat oven to 350°F. Line 22 standard (2½-inch) muffin cups with paper baking cups.

2. Prepare cake mix according to package directions. Spoon batter evenly into prepared muffin cups.

4. Bake 20 minutes or until toothpick inserted into centers comes out clean. Cool in pans 10 minutes. Remove to wire racks; cool completely.

5. Frost cupcakes; top with decorating sugar, if desired. Cut licorice into pieces to fit across cupcakes; cut fruit roll-ups into strips. Decorate as desired to resemble ornaments.

6. Poke two holes in top of each gumdrop with toothpick. Cut licorice into 1½-inch lengths; press into holes to form loops. Press 1 gumdrop into top edge of each cupcake to resemble ornament hanger.   *Makes 22 cupcakes*

Petite Treats

Tropical Coconut Bites

1 jar (24.5 ounces) DOLE® Tropical Fruit
2 cups prepared baking mix
¼ cup apple juice
¼ cup shredded coconut
   Sugar (optional)

• Measure 1½ cups fruit and ¼ cup syrup for recipe. Finely dice fruit.

• Lightly spray 32 miniature muffin cups with vegetable cooking spray.

• Combine baking mix, apple juice, reserved syrup and diced fruit in large mixing bowl, mixing just until combined (mixture will be thick).

• Spoon about 1 tablespoon mixture into each prepared muffin cup. Sprinkle tops with coconut and small amount of sugar, if desired. Bake at 350°F., 12 to 15 minutes or until lightly brown. Remove from pans and cool on wire racks.

Makes 32 servings

Prep Time: 15 minutes • **Bake Time:** 15 minutes

Honey Roasted Peanut Butter Minis

1¼ cups all-purpose flour
1 teaspoon baking powder
¼ teaspoon salt
⅔ cup packed brown sugar
½ cup creamy peanut butter
¼ cup vegetable oil
1 egg
2 tablespoons honey
½ cup milk
⅔ cup chopped honey roasted peanuts, divided
Honey Peanut Butter Frosting (recipe follows)

1. Preheat oven to 350°F. Line 28 mini (1¾-inch) muffin cups with paper baking cups.

2. Combine flour, baking powder and salt in small bowl; mix well. Combine brown sugar, peanut butter, oil, egg and honey in large bowl; stir until smooth and well blended. Add flour mixture and milk; mix just until combined. Stir in ⅓ cup peanuts. Spoon evenly into prepared muffin cups.

3. Bake 15 minutes or until toothpick inserted into centers comes out clean. Cool in pans 5 minutes. Remove to wire racks; cool completely.

4. Prepare Honey Peanut Butter Frosting. Frost cupcakes; sprinkle with remaining ⅓ cup peanuts.   *Makes 28 mini cupcakes*

Honey Peanut Butter Frosting: Combine ⅔ cup creamy peanut butter, ¼ cup (½ stick) softened butter and ¼ cup honey in large bowl; stir until smooth. Stir in 1 cup powdered sugar until well blended.

Taffy Apple Cupcakes

1¾ cups all-purpose flour
1 teaspoon baking soda
1 teaspoon ground cinnamon
½ teaspoon salt
1 cup applesauce
¾ cup sugar
½ cup vegetable oil
1 egg
2¼ cups chopped roasted peanuts
30 wooden craft sticks
3 packages (14 ounces each) caramels, unwrapped
½ cup milk

1. Preheat oven to 350°F. Line 30 mini (1¾-inch) muffin cups with paper baking cups.

2. Combine flour, baking soda, cinnamon and salt in medium bowl; mix well. Combine applesauce, sugar, oil and egg in large bowl; mix well. Add flour mixture; stir until smooth and well blended. Spoon evenly into prepared muffin cups.

3. Bake 15 minutes or until toothpick inserted into centers comes out clean. Cool in pans 5 minutes. Remove to wire racks; cool completely.

4. Line baking sheet with waxed paper; spray with nonstick cooking spray. Place peanuts on plate or in shallow dish. Insert craft sticks into tops of cupcakes.

5. Place caramels and milk in large microwavable bowl; microwave on HIGH 2 to 3 minutes or until melted and smooth, stirring after each minute.

6. Working with one at a time, spoon caramel over cupcake, rotating until completely coated. Immediately roll in peanuts to coat, pressing to adhere. Place on prepared baking sheet. (Caramel may need to be reheated briefly if it becomes too thick.) Let stand 20 minutes or until set. *Makes 30 mini cupcakes*

Lemon Buttons

¾ **cup all-purpose flour**
½ **teaspoon baking powder**
¼ **teaspoon baking soda**
¼ **teaspoon salt**
½ **cup granulated sugar**
¼ **cup (½ stick) butter, softened**
1 **egg**
2½ **tablespoons lemon juice, divided**
¾ **teaspoon grated lemon peel**
¼ **cup milk**
¾ **cup powdered sugar, sifted**
   Pink food coloring
   Yellow sugar pearls

1. Preheat oven to 350°F. Line 30 mini (1¾-inch) muffin cups with paper baking cups.

2. Combine flour, baking powder, baking soda and salt in medium bowl; mix well. Beat granulated sugar and butter in medium bowl with electric mixer at medium speed until creamy. Add egg, 1½ tablespoons lemon juice and lemon peel; beat until well blended. Add flour mixture; beat at low speed while adding milk just until combined. Spoon evenly into prepared muffin cups, filling half full.

3. Bake 10 minutes or until toothpick inserted into centers comes out clean. Cool in pans 5 minutes. Remove to wire racks; cool completely.

4. Whisk powdered sugar and remaining 1 tablespoon lemon juice in small bowl until smooth. Add food coloring, a few drops at a time, until desired shade is reached.

5. Dip tops of cupcakes in glaze to cover completely (coating should be thick); scrape off excess on edge of bowl. Let stand 1 hour or until set.

6. Press 1¼-inch round cookie cutter into tops of cupcakes to score circle in glaze. Arrange sugar pearls in centers of cupcakes to resemble buttonholes.

Makes 30 mini cupcakes

Tip: Filling the muffin cups half full should provide cupcakes that are flat on top (the desired shape to resemble buttons). If your cupcakes have domes after baking, cool them upside down on a sheet of parchment paper to flatten the tops.

Coffee Brownie Bites

1 package (19 to 21 ounces) fudge brownie mix
3 eggs
½ cup vegetable oil
2 teaspoons instant coffee granules
2 teaspoons coffee liqueur (optional)
Powdered sugar (optional)

1. Preheat oven 325°F. Spray 60 mini (1¾-inch) muffin cups with nonstick cooking spray.

2. Combine brownie mix, eggs, oil, coffee granules and coffee liqueur, if desired, in medium bowl; stir until smooth and until well blended. Spoon evenly into prepared muffin cups.

3. Bake 13 minutes or until toothpick inserted into centers comes out almost clean. Remove to wire racks; cool completely.

4. Sprinkle with powdered sugar, if desired. Store in airtight container.

Makes 60 brownie bites

Mini Doughnut Cupcakes

1 cup sugar
1½ teaspoons ground cinnamon
1 package (about 18 ounces) yellow or white cake mix, plus ingredients to prepare mix
1 tablespoon ground nutmeg

1. Preheat oven to 350°F. Grease and flour 60 mini (1¾-inch) muffin cups. Combine sugar and cinnamon in small bowl; set aside.

2. Prepare cake mix according to package directions; stir in nutmeg. Spoon batter evenly into prepared muffin cups.

3. Bake 12 minutes or until lightly browned and toothpick inserted into centers comes out clean.

4. Immediately remove cupcakes from pans. Roll warm cupcakes in sugar-cinnamon mixture until completely coated. Serve warm.   *Makes 60 mini cupcakes*

Tip: Save any remaining sugar-cinnamon mixture to sprinkle on toast and pancakes.

Note: These irresistible little cupcakes allow you to enjoy the lightly spiced flavor of your favorite donuts without all the time and mess it takes to prepare and fry them at home.

Chocolate Caramel Bites

1 cup sugar
¾ cup plus 2 tablespoons all-purpose flour
½ cup unsweetened cocoa powder
¾ teaspoon baking soda
¾ teaspoon baking powder
½ teaspoon salt
½ cup plus 2 tablespoons whole milk, divided
¼ cup vegetable oil
1 egg
½ cup boiling water
24 caramels (about 7 ounces), unwrapped
1 cup semisweet chocolate chips
Colored decors (optional)

1. Preheat oven to 350°F. Line 36 mini (1¾-inch) muffin cups with paper baking cups.

2. Combine sugar, flour, cocoa, baking soda, baking powder and salt in medium bowl; mix well. Beat ½ cup milk, oil and egg in large bowl with electric mixer at medium speed until well blended. Add sugar mixture; beat 2 minutes. Add water; beat at low speed until well blended. (Batter will be thin.) Spoon evenly into prepared muffin cups. Bake 8 minutes.

3. Meanwhile, combine caramels and remaining 2 tablespoons milk in medium microwavable bowl. Microwave on HIGH 1½ minutes; stir. Microwave at 30-second intervals until melted and smooth, stirring after each interval.

4. Spoon ½ teaspoon caramel sauce over each partially baked cupcake. Bake 4 minutes or until toothpick inserted near edges of cupcakes comes out clean. Cool in pans 10 minutes. Remove to wire racks; cool completely.

5. Place chocolate chips in small microwavable bowl. Microwave on HIGH 1 minute; stir. Microwave at additional 15-second intervals until chocolate is melted. Reheat remaining caramel sauce in microwave until melted; drizzle chocolate and caramel sauce over cupcakes. Top with decors, if desired. *Makes 36 mini cupcakes*

Carrot Cake Minis

1 cup packed light brown sugar
¾ cup plus 2 tablespoons all-purpose flour
1 teaspoon baking soda
½ teaspoon salt
½ teaspoon ground cinnamon
¼ teaspoon ground nutmeg
⅛ teaspoon ground cloves
½ cup canola oil
2 eggs, lightly beaten
1½ cups lightly packed grated carrots
½ teaspoon vanilla
    Cream Cheese Frosting (recipe follows)
    Toasted shredded coconut (optional)*

To toast coconut, spread evenly on ungreased baking sheet. Bake in preheated 350°F oven 5 to 7 minutes or until light golden brown, stirring occasionally.

1. Preheat oven to 350°F. Line 36 mini (1¾-inch) muffin cups with paper baking cups.

2. Combine brown sugar, flour, baking soda, salt, cinnamon, nutmeg and cloves in large bowl; mix well. Add oil; stir until blended. Add eggs, one at a time, stirring until blended after each addition. Stir in carrots and vanilla. Spoon evenly into prepared muffin cups.

3. Bake 15 minutes or until toothpick inserted into centers comes out clean. Cool in pans 5 minutes. Remove to wire racks; cool completely.

4. Prepare Cream Cheese Frosting. Frost cupcakes; sprinkle with toasted coconut. Serve immediately or cover and refrigerate until ready to serve.

Makes 36 mini cupcakes

Cream Cheese Frosting: Beat 1 package (8 ounces) softened cream cheese and ¼ cup (½ stick) softened butter in medium bowl with electric mixer at medium-high speed until creamy. Beat in ¼ teaspoon salt and ¼ teaspoon vanilla. Beat in 1½ cups sifted powdered sugar until well blended.

Mojito Minis

Cupcakes
- ¾ cup all-purpose flour
- ½ teaspoon baking powder
- ½ teaspoon baking soda
- ¼ teaspoon salt
- ½ cup granulated sugar
- ¼ cup (½ stick) butter, softened
- 1 egg
- Grated peel and juice of 1 lime
- ¼ cup milk
- 2 to 4 tablespoons white rum, divided
- ¼ cup chopped fresh mint

Frosting
- 2½ cups powdered sugar
- Juice of 2 limes
- ¾ cup (1½ sticks) butter, softened
- 2 tablespoons chopped fresh mint
- Small whole fresh mint leaves (optional)

1. Preheat oven to 350°F. Line 18 mini (1¾-inch) muffin cups with paper baking cups.

2. Combine flour, baking powder, baking soda and salt in small bowl; mix well. Beat granulated sugar and ¼ cup butter in large bowl with electric mixer at medium speed until fluffy. Add egg, peel and juice of 1 lime; beat until well blended. Add flour mixture, milk and 2 tablespoons rum; beat just until combined. Stir in ¼ cup mint. Spoon evenly into prepared muffin cups.

3. Bake 15 minutes or until toothpick inserted into centers comes out clean. Brush warm cupcakes with remaining 2 tablespoons rum, if desired. Remove to wire racks; cool completely.

4. Beat powdered sugar and juice of 2 limes in large bowl with electric mixer at medium speed until well blended. Add ¾ cup butter; beat at high speed 3 minutes or until thick and fluffy. Stir in 2 tablespoons mint. Frost cupcakes; garnish with mint leaves.

Makes 18 mini cupcakes

Triple Chocolate PB Minis

2 packages (about 4½ ounces each) chocolate peanut butter cups, chopped, divided*

1 package (about 18 ounces) chocolate fudge cake mix, plus ingredients to prepare mix

¾ cup whipping cream

1½ cups semisweet chocolate chips

*Refrigerate or freeze candy ahead of time to make chopping easier.

1. Preheat oven to 350°F. Line 60 mini (1¾-inch) muffin cups with paper baking cups.

2. Prepare cake mix according to package directions; stir in 1 cup chopped peanut butter cups. Spoon batter evenly into prepared muffin cups.

3. Bake 10 minutes or until toothpick inserted into centers comes out clean. Cool in pans 5 minutes. Remove to wire racks; cool completely.

4. Bring cream to a simmer in small saucepan over medium heat. Place chocolate chips in medium heatproof bowl. Pour hot cream over chocolate chips; let stand 2 minutes. Whisk mixture until chocolate is melted and mixture is smooth. Dip tops of cupcakes in chocolate mixture; return to wire racks. Let stand 10 minutes; dip tops again, if desired. Sprinkle with remaining peanut butter cups. Let stand until set.

Makes 60 mini cupcakes

Tangy Raspberry Minis

    1 cup all-purpose flour
    ½ teaspoon baking powder
    ½ teaspoon baking soda
    ½ cup granulated sugar
    ¼ cup (½ stick) butter, softened
    1 egg
    ½ teaspoon vanilla
    ½ cup buttermilk
    24 fresh raspberries
    2 tablespoons coarse sugar
    2 cups powdered sugar
    6 to 9 tablespoons milk, divided

1. Preheat oven to 350°F. Line 24 mini (1¾-inch) muffin cups with paper baking cups.

2. Combine flour, baking powder and baking soda in small bowl; mix well. Beat granulated sugar and butter in large bowl with electric mixer at medium speed until creamy. Add egg and vanilla; beat until well blended. Add flour mixture and buttermilk; beat at low speed until just combined. Spoon evenly into prepared muffin cups. Top each cup with 1 raspberry. Sprinkle evenly with coarse sugar.

3. Bake 15 minutes or until golden brown. Cool in pans 5 minutes. Remove to wire racks; cool completely.

4. Whisk powdered sugar and 6 tablespoons milk in medium bowl until smooth. Add remaining milk, 1 tablespoon at a time, to make pourable glaze. Drizzle over cupcakes. *Makes 24 mini cupcakes*

Mini Fruitcake Cupcakes

1½ cups dried fruit (raisins, cherries, cranberries, dates, chopped figs or apricots)
½ cup Port wine or orange juice
¾ cup all-purpose flour
½ teaspoon *each* **baking powder, ground ginger and ground cinnamon**
¼ teaspoon *each* **salt and ground allspice**
⅓ cup granulated sugar
5 tablespoons butter
¼ cup packed light brown sugar
2 eggs
2 tablespoons orange juice
1 teaspoon finely grated orange peel
½ cup chopped pecans, toasted*
1 cup powdered sugar
3 tablespoons lemon juice

*To toast pecans, spread in single layer on baking sheet. Bake in preheated 350°F oven 5 to 7 minutes or until golden brown, stirring frequently.

1. Preheat oven to 350°F. Line 28 mini (1¾-inch) muffin cups with paper baking cups.

2. Combine dried fruit and Port wine in medium microwavable bowl. Cover and microwave on HIGH 1 minute. Stir; microwave 1 minute. Let stand 15 minutes or until cool.

3. Combine flour, baking powder, ginger, cinnamon, salt and allspice in medium bowl; mix well. Beat granulated sugar, butter and brown sugar in large bowl with electric mixer at medium speed until creamy. Add eggs, one at a time, beating until well blended after each addition. Add orange juice and orange peel; beat until blended. Gradually add flour mixture, beating until well blended after each addition. Stir in fruit with wine and pecans. Spoon evenly into prepared muffin cups.

4. Bake 15 minutes or until toothpick inserted into centers comes out clean. Cool in pans 5 minutes. Remove to wire racks.

5. Whisk powdered sugar and lemon juice in small bowl until smooth. Brush glaze over tops of warm cupcakes. Cool completely.   *Makes 28 mini cupcakes*

Tip: If you don't have mini muffin pans, arrange mini foil baking cups on ungreased cookie sheets. Fill and bake as directed, being careful to spoon batter into the center of the cups so they do not tip over.

Kiddie Creations

Meteorite Mini Cakes

1 package (about 18 ounces) chocolate cake mix, plus ingredients to prepare mix
2 containers (16 ounces each) vanilla frosting
   Red, green, blue and yellow food coloring
1 bag (11 ounces) chocolate chunks

1. Preheat oven to 350°F. Spray 12 standard (2½-inch) muffin cups with nonstick cooking spray.

2. Prepare cake mix according to package directions. Spoon batter evenly into prepared muffin cups. Bake 20 minutes or until toothpick inserted into centers comes out clean. Cool in pan 10 minutes. Remove to wire rack; cool completely.

3. Trim cupcake edges to form rounded shapes. Microwave frosting in medium microwavable bowl on LOW (30%) 30 seconds or until melted. Divide frosting among four small bowls. Add food coloring, a few drops at a time, until desired shades are reached. Pour half of each color frosting over cupcakes, coating completely. Refrigerate cakes 20 minutes.

4. Press chocolate chunks into frosting. Reheat remaining frosting on LOW (30%) 30 seconds or until melted. Coat cupcakes again. Cover and refrigerate until ready to serve.   *Makes 12 cakes*

Letter Cupcakes

3 cups all-purpose flour
2 teaspoons baking powder
½ teaspoon salt
1½ cups sugar
½ cup (1 stick) butter, softened
2 eggs
1 teaspoon vanilla
1 cup sour cream
1 container (16 ounces) white frosting
Jumbo red nonpareils

1. Preheat oven to 350°F. Line 24 standard (2½-inch) muffin cups with paper baking cups.

2. Combine flour, baking powder and salt in medium bowl; mix well. Beat sugar and butter in large bowl with electric mixer at medium speed 2 to 3 minutes or until light and fluffy. Add eggs, one at a time, beating well after each addition. Stir in vanilla. Alternately add flour mixture with sour cream, beating until just blended. Spoon evenly into prepared muffin cups.

3. Bake 20 to 25 minutes or until toothpick inserted into centers comes out clean. Cool in pans 10 minutes. Remove to wire racks; cool completely.

4. Place frosting in medium microwavable bowl; microwave on HIGH 10 to 15 seconds or until slightly melted. Dip tops of cupcakes in frosting to coat; return to wire racks. Place nonpareils on cupcakes to create letters and words. Let stand until set.

Makes 24 cupcakes

Blue Suede Cupcakes

2¼ cups all-purpose flour
1 teaspoon salt
2 bottles (1 ounce each) blue food coloring
3 tablespoons unsweetened cocoa powder
1 cup buttermilk
1 teaspoon vanilla
1½ cups granulated sugar
1 cup (2 sticks) butter, softened, divided
2 eggs
1 teaspoon white vinegar
1 teaspoon baking soda
1 package (8 ounces) cream cheese, softened
3 cups powdered sugar
2 tablespoons milk
    Additional blue food coloring
    Blue decorating sugar

1. Preheat oven to 350°F. Line 20 standard (2½-inch) muffin cups with paper baking cups.

2. Combine flour and salt in medium bowl; mix well. Gradually stir 2 bottles food coloring into cocoa in small bowl until smooth and well blended. Combine buttermilk and vanilla in another small bowl.

3. Beat granulated sugar and ½ cup butter in large bowl with electric mixer at medium speed 4 minutes or until light and fluffy. Add eggs, one at a time, beating well after each addition. Add cocoa mixture; beat until well blended and uniform in color. Alternately add flour mixture and buttermilk mixture, beating well after each addition. Stir vinegar into baking soda in small bowl; gently stir into batter (do not use mixer). Spoon evenly into prepared muffin cups.

4. Bake 20 minutes or until toothpick inserted into centers comes out clean. Cool in pans 10 minutes. Remove to wire racks; cool completely.

5. Beat remaining ½ cup butter and cream cheese in another large bowl with electric mixer at medium-high speed until smooth. Gradually beat in powdered sugar at low speed. Beat in milk until blended. Add additional food coloring, a few drops at a time, until desired shade is reached. Frost cupcakes; sprinkle with decorating sugar.

Makes 20 cupcakes

Pink Piglets

1 package (about 18 ounces) yellow cake mix, plus ingredients to prepare mix
Pink or red food coloring
1 container (16 ounces) white frosting
Mini semisweet chocolate chips
Small fruit-flavored pastel candy wafers
Red or pink chewy fruit candy squares

1. Preheat oven to 350°F. Line 60 mini (1¾-inch) muffin cups with paper baking cups.

2. Prepare cake mix according to package directions. Spoon batter evenly into prepared muffin cups.

3. Bake 10 minutes or until toothpick inserted into centers comes out clean. Cool in pans 10 minutes. Remove to wire racks; cool completely.

4. Add food coloring to frosting, a few drops at a time, until desired shade is reached. Frost cupcakes.

5. Create faces at one side of each cupcake using chocolate chips for eyes and candy wafers for noses.

6. Working with one at a time, unwrap candy squares and microwave on LOW (30%) 5 to 10 seconds or until softened. Press candy between hands or on waxed paper to flatten to ⅛-inch thickness. Using scissors or paring knife, cut out triangles for ears; fold over top corner of each triangle. Arrange ears on cupcakes.

7. Cut ⅛-inch strips, 1 to 2 inches long, from flattened candies. Shape candy strips into spirals for tails; place candies in freezer 10 minutes to set. Place tails on cupcakes. *Makes 60 mini cupcakes*

Sunny Side Upcakes

1 package (about 18 ounces) vanilla cake mix, plus ingredients to prepare mix
2 containers (16 ounces each) white frosting
22 yellow chewy fruit candy squares

1. Preheat oven to 350°F. Line 22 standard (2½-inch) muffin cups with paper baking cups.

2. Prepare cake mix according to package directions. Spoon batter evenly into prepared muffin cups.

3. Bake 20 minutes or until toothpick inserted into centers comes out clean. Cool in pans 10 minutes. Remove to wire racks; cool completely.

4. Place 1 cup frosting in small microwavable bowl; microwave on LOW (30%) 10 seconds or until slightly melted. Working with one cupcake at a time, spoon about 2 tablespoons frosting in center of top of cupcake. Spread frosting toward edges of cupcake in uneven petal shape to resemble egg white.

5. Unwrap 1 candy square and microwave on LOW (30%) 5 seconds or just until softened. Shape into ball; flatten slightly. Press candy into frosting in center of cupcake to resemble egg yolk. *Makes 22 cupcakes*

Grape Soda Cupcakes

1½ cups all-purpose flour
1 envelope (0.15-ounce) grape unsweetened drink mix
2 teaspoons baking powder
⅛ teaspoon salt
1 cup granulated sugar
1 cup (2 sticks) unsalted butter, softened, divided
2 eggs
½ cup plus 3 tablespoons milk, divided
1½ teaspoons vanilla, divided
3 cups powdered sugar
Purple gel food coloring
Pearl decors (optional)

1. Preheat oven to 350°F. Line 12 standard (2½-inch) muffin cups with paper baking cups.

2. Combine flour, drink mix, baking powder and salt in small bowl; mix well. Beat granulated sugar and ½ cup butter in medium bowl with electric mixer at medium speed until creamy. Add eggs, one at a time, beating well after each addition. Add flour mixture; beat until well blended. Add ½ cup milk and 1 teaspoon vanilla; beat until smooth. Spoon evenly into prepared muffin cups.

3. Bake 20 minutes or until toothpick inserted into centers comes out clean. Cool in pan 10 minutes. Remove to wire rack; cool completely.

4. Beat powdered sugar, remaining ½ cup butter, 3 tablespoons milk and ½ teaspoon vanilla in large bowl with electric mixer at medium speed until fluffy. Add food coloring, a few drops at a time, until desired shade is reached.

5. Frost cupcakes; top with decors, if desired.   *Makes 12 cupcakes*

Friendly Frogs

1 package (about 18 ounces) cake mix, any flavor, plus ingredients to prepare mix
Green food coloring
1 container (16 ounces) white frosting
Green decorating sugar (optional)
Black round candies or candy-coated chocolate pieces
White chocolate candy discs
Black and red string licorice
Green jelly candy fruit slices (optional)

1. Preheat oven to 350°F. Line 22 standard (2½-inch) muffin cups with paper baking cups.

2. Prepare cake mix according to package directions. Spoon batter evenly into prepared muffin cups.

3. Bake 20 minutes or until toothpick inserted into centers comes out clean. Cool in pans 10 minutes. Remove to wire racks; cool completely.

4. Add food coloring to frosting, a few drops at a time, until desired shade is reached. Frost cupcakes; sprinkle with decorating sugar, if desired.

5. Use small dab of frosting to attach black candies to white discs for eyes. Cut licorice into shorter lengths for noses and mouths. Arrange candies on cupcakes for frog faces.

6. Using scissors, cut jelly candies into feet, if desired. Place cupcakes on candy feet just before serving.
Makes 22 cupcakes

Leopard Spots

1 package (about 18 ounces) dark chocolate cake mix, plus ingredients
    to prepare mix
3 cups powdered sugar, sifted
½ cup (1 stick) butter, softened
2 to 4 tablespoons milk, divided
½ teaspoon vanilla
    Brown and yellow food coloring
    Black and orange decorating gels

1. Preheat oven to 350°F. Line 24 standard (2½-inch) muffin cups with paper baking cups.

2. Prepare cake mix according to package directions. Spoon batter evenly into prepared muffin cups.

3. Bake 20 minutes or until toothpick inserted into centers comes out clean. Cool in pans 10 minutes. Remove to wire racks; cool completely.

4. Beat powdered sugar, butter, 2 tablespoons milk and vanilla in large bowl with electric mixer at low speed until blended. Beat at high speed until light and fluffy, adding additional milk, 1 teaspoon at a time, until desired spreading consistency is reached. Add food coloring, a few drops at a time, until desired shade is reached.

5. Frost cupcakes; pipe spots all over tops of cupcakes using black decorating gel for outline and orange decorating gel in centers.
        Makes 24 cupcakes

Crazy Colors Cupcakes

1 package (about 18 ounces) white cake mix
1 cup sour cream
3 eggs
½ cup vegetable oil
   Gel food coloring (4 colors)
1 container (16 ounces) white or cream cheese frosting
   Mini rainbow candy-coated chocolate chips

1. Preheat oven to 325°F. Line 20 standard (2½-inch) muffin cups with white paper baking cups.

2. Beat cake mix, sour cream, eggs and oil in large bowl with electric mixer at low speed 30 seconds. Beat at medium speed 2 minutes or until well blended. Divide batter evenly among four medium bowls. Stir food coloring into each bowl, a few drops at a time, until well blended and uniform in color. (Batter colors should be strong to retain color after baking.)

3. Spoon 2 teaspoons of one color batter into each prepared cup; spread to edge of cup with back of spoon or dampened fingers. Top with second color batter, making sure to completely cover first layer. Repeat with remaining two colors of batter. (If desired, switch order of colored layers halfway though assembly.)

4. Bake 18 to 20 minutes or until toothpick inserted into centers comes out clean. Cool in pans 10 minutes. Remove to wire racks; cool completely.

5. Frost cupcakes; decorate with rainbow chips.   *Makes 20 cupcakes*

Tip: Use as few or as many colors as you like for the rainbow layers and adjust the amount of batter in each cup accordingly.

Nuclear Blasted Cupcakes

1 package (8 ounces) cream cheese, softened
1 egg
⅓ cup granulated sugar
5 to 6 drops neon or assorted food colors, any color
1 cup semi-sweet chocolate pieces or chunks
1 box (18.25 ounces) white or vanilla cake mix
⅓ cup vegetable oil
3 eggs
V8® Splash Tropical Blend Juice
1 can (16 ounces) vanilla frosting
Colored sugar

1. Heat the oven to 350°F. Put baking cup liners into **24** (2½-inch) muffin-pan cups.

2. Stir the cream cheese, egg and granulated sugar in a 2-quart bowl until well blended. Stir in the food coloring. Add the chocolate pieces and set the mixture aside.

3. Prepare the cake mix following the package directions using the oil and eggs, and substituting an equal amount of juice for the water. Spoon the batter evenly into the prepared muffin-pan cups. Put **about 1 tablespoon** of the cream cheese mixture on the center of the batter of each filled muffin-pan cup.

4. Bake for 25 minutes or until a toothpick inserted in the center of a cupcake comes out clean. Remove the cupcakes from the pan and cool them on a wire rack.

5. Frost the cooled cupcakes with the frosting and sprinkle with colored sugar.

Makes 24 cupcakes

Campbell's Kitchen Tip: I like to use a **½ cup** measuring cup or ice cream scoop to portion the batter into the muffin-pan cups so all my cupcakes come out the same size.

Prep Time: 30 minutes • **Bake Time:** 25 minutes • **Cool Time:** 1 hour

Cupcake Sliders

    2 cups all-purpose flour
2½ teaspoons baking powder
   ½ teaspoon salt
    1 cup milk
   ½ teaspoon vanilla
1½ cups sugar
   ½ cup (1 stick) butter, softened
    3 eggs
1¼ cups chocolate hazelnut spread or milk chocolate frosting
     Colored decors (optional)

1. Preheat oven to 350°F. Spray 18 standard (2½-inch) muffin cups with nonstick cooking spray.

2. Combine flour, baking powder and salt in medium bowl; mix well. Combine milk and vanilla in small bowl. Beat sugar and butter in large bowl with electric mixer at medium speed 3 minutes or until creamy. Add eggs, one at a time, beating well after each addition. Alternately add flour mixture and milk mixture, beating well after each addition. Spoon evenly into prepared muffin cups.

3. Bake 18 to 20 minutes or until toothpick inserted into centers comes out clean. Cool in pans 10 minutes. Remove to wire racks; cool completely.

4. Cut off edges of cupcakes to form squares. Cut cupcakes in half crosswise. Spread each bottom half with about 1 tablespoon chocolate hazelnut spread; sprinkle with decors, if desired. Replace tops of cupcakes.   *Makes 18 cupcakes*

Pretty in Pink

2 cups all-purpose flour
1 teaspoon baking soda
1 teaspoon baking powder
½ teaspoon salt
½ cup sour cream
½ cup milk
1 teaspoon vanilla
1 cup granulated sugar
½ cup (1 stick) butter, softened
2 eggs
2 to 3 tablespoons multi-colored cake decors (sprinkles)
  Pink food coloring
1 container (16 ounces) white frosting
  White and pink decorating sugars
12 small tiaras

1. Preheat oven to 350°F. Line 12 standard (2½-inch) muffin cups with paper baking cups.

2. Combine flour, baking soda, baking powder and salt in medium bowl; mix well. Stir sour cream, milk and vanilla in small bowl until well blended. Beat granulated sugar and butter in large bowl with electric mixer at medium speed 2 minutes or until fluffy. Add eggs, one at a time, beating well after each addition. Alternately add flour mixture and sour cream mixture, beating well after each addition. Stir in decors until well blended. Spoon evenly into prepared muffin cups.

3. Bake 20 to 22 minutes or until toothpick inserted into centers comes out clean. Cool in pan 10 minutes. Remove to wire rack; cool completely.

4. Add food coloring to frosting, a few drops at a time, until desired shade is reached.

5. Frost cupcakes; sprinkle with decorating sugars. Arrange tiaras on cupcakes.

Makes 12 cupcakes

Zebra Stripes

1 package (about 18 ounces) dark chocolate cake mix, plus ingredients to prepare mix
8 ounces whipping cream
24 ounces white chocolate, chopped
Black decorating icing

1. Preheat oven to 350°F. Line 24 standard (2½-inch) muffin cups with paper baking cups.

2. Prepare cake mix according to package directions. Spoon batter evenly into prepared muffin cups.

3. Bake 20 minutes or until toothpick inserted into centers comes out clean. Cool in pans 10 minutes. Remove to wire racks; cool completely.

4. Bring cream to a simmer in small saucepan over medium heat. Place chopped white chocolate in medium heatproof bowl. Pour hot cream over white chocolate; let stand 2 minutes. Whisk mixture until white chocolate is melted and mixture is smooth. Dip tops of cupcakes in white chocolate mixture; return to wire racks. Let stand 10 minutes; dip tops again, if desired. Let stand until set.

5. Pipe stripes on tops of cupcakes with decorating icing.   *Makes 24 cupcakes*

Furry Monsters

Cupcakes
- 1½ cups all-purpose flour
- 1 teaspoon baking powder
- ½ teaspoon baking soda
- ½ teaspoon salt
- 1 cup granulated sugar
- ½ cup (1 stick) butter, softened
- 2 eggs
- Grated peel and juice of 1 lemon
- ½ cup buttermilk

Frosting
- 2½ cups powdered sugar
- Juice of 2 lemons
- 2 tablespoons boiling water
- ¼ teaspoon salt
- ¾ cup (1½ sticks) butter, softened
- Green food coloring
- Assorted candies and black string licorice
- Black decorating gel

1. Preheat oven to 350°F. Line 12 standard (2½-inch) muffin cups with paper baking cups.

2. Combine flour, baking powder, baking soda and ½ teaspoon salt in medium bowl; mix well. Beat granulated sugar and ½ cup butter in large bowl with electric mixer at medium speed until creamy. Add eggs, peel and juice of 1 lemon; beat until well blended. Add flour mixture; beat at low speed while adding buttermilk until just combined. Spoon evenly into prepared muffin cups.

3. Bake 20 to 22 minutes or until toothpick inserted into centers comes out clean. Cool in pan 5 minutes. Remove to wire rack; cool completely.

4. Beat powdered sugar, juice of 2 lemons, boiling water and ¼ teaspoon salt in large bowl with electric mixer at low speed until cool. Add ¾ cup butter; beat at medium-high speed 3 minutes or until doubled in volume. Add food coloring, a few drops at a time, until desired shade is reached.

5. Place frosting in piping bag fitted with star tip; pipe frosting on cupcakes to resemble fur. Decorate with candies and licorice to create monster faces. Pipe dot of decorating gel in each eye. *Makes 12 cupcakes*

Mini Bees

1 package (about 18 ounces) chocolate cake mix, plus ingredients to prepare mix
1 container (16 ounces) chocolate frosting
1½ cups prepared white frosting
Yellow food coloring
Black string licorice
Yellow candy wafers

1. Preheat oven to 350°F. Line 60 mini (1¾-inch) muffin cups with paper baking cups.

2. Prepare cake mix according to package directions. Spoon batter evenly into prepared muffin cups.

3. Bake 10 minutes or until toothpick inserted into centers comes out clean. Cool in pans 5 minutes. Remove to wire racks; cool completely.

4. Place chocolate frosting in medium microwavable bowl. Microwave on LOW (30%) 30 seconds; stir until melted. Dip tops of cupcakes in melted frosting to coat; place on baking sheet. (Frosting may need to be reheated several times to maintain melted consistency.) Refrigerate 10 minutes or until frosting is set. Reserve remaining chocolate frosting.

5. Place white frosting in medium bowl; add food coloring, a few drops at a time, until desired shade is reached. Place in piping bag fitted with small round tip or resealable food storage bag with ¼-inch corner cut off. Pipe stripes on cupcakes.

6. Place reserved chocolate frosting in separate piping bag fitted with small round tip or resealable food storage bag with ¼-inch corner cut off. Pipe eyes and mouths on cupcakes.

7. Cut licorice into 1½-inch lengths; place on cupcakes just above eyes for antennae and at opposite side for stingers. Cut candy wafers in half; arrange two halves on each cupcake for wings. *Makes 60 mini cupcakes*

6. Spoon frosting into piping bags with round decorating tips or small food storage bags with small corners cut off. Pipe shirts on dolls; smooth with spatula or finger. Pipe border around dolls' waists to cover seam between shirt and skirt. Transfer to serving plates or large tray. Pipe border around bottom of cupcakes. Pipe flowers (or desired decorations) on skirts; press 1 nonpareil into center of each flower.

Makes 12 princesses

Tip: If using dolls rather than doll picks, remove the dolls' clothing and wrap the hair in plastic wrap to keep it clean while decorating.

Beyond Basic Bites

Cheesecake Cookie Cups

1 package (16.5 ounces) NESTLÉ® TOLL HOUSE® Refrigerated Chocolate Chip Cookie Bar Dough
2 packages (8 ounces each) cream cheese, at room temperature
1 can (14 ounces) NESTLÉ® CARNATION® Sweetened Condensed Milk
2 large eggs
2 teaspoons vanilla extract
1 can (21 ounces) cherry pie filling

PREHEAT oven to 325°F. Paper-line 24 muffin cups. Place one piece of cookie dough in each muffin cup.

BAKE for 10 to 12 minutes or until cookie has spread to edge of cup.

BEAT cream cheese, sweetened condensed milk, eggs and vanilla extract in medium bowl until smooth. Pour about 3 tablespoons cream cheese mixture over each cookie in cup.

BAKE for additional 15 to 18 minutes or until set. Cool completely in pan on wire rack. Top each with level tablespoon of pie filling. Refrigerate for 1 hour.

Makes 2 dozen cookie cups

Prep Time: 15 minutes • **Baking Time:** 25 minutes • **Cooling Time:** 1 hour refrigerating

Raspberry Layer Cupcakes

       2 cups all-purpose flour
    2½ teaspoons baking powder
     ½ teaspoon salt
       1 cup milk
       1 teaspoon vanilla
    1½ cups granulated sugar
     ½ cup (1 stick) butter, softened
       3 eggs
    1½ cups seedless raspberry jam
       Powdered sugar

1. Preheat oven to 350°F. Spray 18 standard (2½-inch) muffin cups with nonstick cooking spray.

2. Combine flour, baking powder and salt in medium bowl; mix well. Whisk milk and vanilla in small bowl. Beat granulated sugar and butter in large bowl with electric mixer at medium speed 3 minutes or until creamy. Add eggs, one at a time, beating well after each addition. Alternately add flour mixture with milk mixture, beating until well blended. Spoon evenly into prepared muffin cups.

3. Bake 18 to 20 minutes or until toothpick inserted into centers comes out clean. Cool in pans 10 minutes. Remove to wire racks; cool completely.

4. Working with one at a time, cut cupcake in thirds crosswise. Spread about 2 teaspoons jam over bottom layer. Top with second layer; spread with 2 teaspoons jam. Top with third layer. Repeat with remaining cupcakes and jam. Sprinkle with powdered sugar.

Makes 18 cupcakes

Quick Cookie Cupcakes

1 package (about 16 ounces) refrigerated break-apart chocolate chip cookie dough (24 count)
1½ cups prepared chocolate frosting
Colored decors

1. Preheat oven to 350°F. Line 24 mini (1¾-inch) muffin cups with paper baking cups.

2. Break dough into 24 pieces along score lines. Roll each piece into a ball; place in prepared muffin cups.

3. Bake 10 to 12 minutes or until golden brown. Cool in pans 5 minutes. Remove to wire racks; cool completely.

4. Frost cupcakes; sprinkle with decors. *Makes 24 mini cupcakes*

Party Ice Cream Cupcakes

1 box (12-ounce) prepared pound cake
1 container (1.5 quarts) BREYERS® All Natural Mint Chocolate Chip or Chocolate Ice Cream
½ cup rainbow colored sprinkles

Line 12-cup muffin pan with cupcake liners; set aside. Trim off top of cake to flatten. Cut cake horizontally into 3 slices, then cut out 12 rounds using 2¼-inch round cookie cutter or glass; arrange 1 cake round in each muffin cup.

Scoop BREYERS® All Natural Mint Chocolate Chip Ice Cream onto cakes, then roll in sprinkles. Freeze 2 hours or until firm. *Makes 12 servings*

Prep Time: 30 minutes • **Freeze Time:** 2 hours

Whoopie Pie Cupcakes

1 package (about 18 ounces) dark chocolate cake mix, plus ingredients to prepare mix
½ cup (1 stick) butter, softened
¼ cup shortening
3 cups powdered sugar
⅓ cup whipping cream
1 teaspoon salt

1. Preheat oven to 350°F. Grease 24 standard (2½-inch) muffin cups.

2. Prepare cake mix according to package directions. Spoon batter evenly into prepared muffin cups.

3. Bake 20 minutes or until toothpick inserted into centers comes out clean. Cool in pans 10 minutes. Remove to wire racks; cool completely.

4. Beat butter and shortening in large bowl with electric mixer at medium speed until well blended. Add powdered sugar, cream and salt; beat at low speed 1 minute. Beat at medium-high speed 2 minutes or until fluffy.

5. Slice tops off cupcakes. Spread filling over bottoms of cupcakes; replace tops.

Makes 24 cupcakes

Truffle Brownie Bites

¾ cup plus ⅔ cup semisweet chocolate chips, divided
½ cup (1 stick) butter, cut into chunks
1⅓ cups sugar
3 eggs
1 teaspoon vanilla
1 cup minus 2 tablespoons all-purpose flour
½ teaspoon salt
¼ cup plus 2 tablespoons whipping cream
Colored sprinkles

1. Preheat oven to 350°F. Line 36 mini (1¾-inch) muffin cups with paper baking cups.

2. Combine ⅔ cup chocolate chips and butter in large microwavable bowl. Microwave on HIGH 30 seconds; stir. Repeat at 10-second intervals until chocolate chips are melted and mixture is smooth. Let stand to cool slightly.

3. Add sugar to chocolate mixture; beat until well blended. Add eggs, one at a time, beating well after each addition. Stir in vanilla. Add flour and salt; beat until well blended. Spoon evenly into prepared muffin cups.

4. Bake 15 minutes or until tops are firm. Cool in pans 5 minutes. Remove to wire racks; cool completely.

5. Bring cream to a simmer in small saucepan over medium heat. Place remaining ¾ cup chocolate chips in medium heatproof bowl. Pour hot cream over chocolate chips; let stand 2 minutes. Whisk mixture until chocolate is melted and mixture is smooth. Dip tops of cupcakes in chocolate mixture; return to wire racks. Let stand 10 minutes; dip tops again, if desired. Decorate with sprinkles. Let stand until set.

Makes 36 brownie bites

Crispy Cupcakes

¼ cup (½ stick) plus 2 tablespoons butter, divided
1 package (10½ ounces) marshmallows
½ cup creamy peanut butter
6 cups crisp rice cereal
1 cup bittersweet or semisweet chocolate chips
1½ cups powdered sugar
¼ cup milk

1. Spray 13×9-inch baking pan with nonstick cooking spray.

2. Microwave 2 tablespoons butter in large microwavable bowl on HIGH 30 seconds or until melted. Add marshmallows; stir until evenly coated. Microwave on HIGH 1 minute; stir. Microwave 45 seconds; stir until melted and smooth. Stir in peanut butter until well blended. Add cereal; stir until blended.

3. Spread mixture in prepared pan, using waxed paper to spread and press into even layer. Let stand 10 to 15 minutes or until set.

4. Meanwhile, place remaining ¼ cup butter and chocolate chips in medium microwavable bowl. Microwave on HIGH 40 seconds; stir. Microwave at additional 15-second intervals until melted and smooth. Gradually beat in powdered sugar and milk until well blended. Refrigerate until ready to use.

5. Spray 1½-inch round cookie or biscuit cutter with nonstick cooking spray; cut out 36 circles from cereal. Place small dab of frosting on top of 18 circles; top with remaining 18 circles, pressing mixture down firmly. Place in paper baking cups, if desired.

6. Place remaining chocolate frosting in pastry bag fitted with small round tip; pipe frosting on top of cupcakes. *Makes 18 cupcakes*

Marshmallow Fudge Sundae Cupcakes

- 1 package (about 18 ounces) chocolate cake mix, plus ingredients to prepare mix
- 2 packages (4 ounces each) waffle bowls
- 20 large marshmallows
- 1 jar (8 ounces) hot fudge topping
- Colored sprinkles
- 1¼ cups whipped topping
- 1 jar (10 ounces) maraschino cherries

1. Preheat oven to 350°F. Spray 20 standard (2½-inch) muffin cups with nonstick cooking spray.

2. Prepare cake mix according to package directions. Spoon batter evenly into prepared muffin cups.

3. Bake 20 minutes or until toothpick inserted into centers comes out clean. Cool in pans 10 minutes. Remove to wire racks; cool completely.

4. Place waffle bowls on ungreased baking sheets. Place 1 cupcake in each waffle bowl. Top each cupcake with 1 marshmallow.

5. Bake 2 minutes or until marshmallows are slightly softened.

6. Remove lid from hot fudge topping; microwave on HIGH 10 seconds or until softened.

7. Top each cupcake with hot fudge topping, sprinkles, whipped topping and 1 cherry. Serve immediately.   *Makes 20 servings*

Little Strawberry Cookie Cakes

1 pound fresh strawberries, stems removed
⅓ cup sugar
1 teaspoon vanilla
3 cups whipping cream
1 (9-ounce) box chocolate wafers

1. Line 12 standard (2½-inch) muffin cups with foil baking cups. Reserve 6 strawberries; set aside.

2. Place remaining strawberries, sugar and vanilla in food processor or blender; process using on/off pulsing action until strawberries are finely chopped.

3. Beat cream in large bowl with electric mixer on medium speed until stiff peaks form; fold into strawberry mixture.

4. Place 1 wafer in bottom of each prepared muffin cup. Spoon about 1 tablespoon of strawberry mixture onto wafers; top with remaining wafers. Top each with about 1 tablespoon strawberry mixture. Cover and refrigerate at least 6 hours or up to 24 hours.

5. Slice reserved 6 strawberries in half; top each cake with one strawberry half.

Makes 12 servings

Mini Cocoa Cupcake Kabobs

1 cup sugar
1 cup all-purpose flour
⅓ cup HERSHEY®'S Cocoa
¾ teaspoon baking powder
¾ teaspoon baking soda
½ teaspoon salt
1 egg
½ cup milk
¼ cup vegetable oil
1 teaspoon vanilla extract
½ cup boiling water
LICKETY-SPLIT COCOA FROSTING (page 239)
Jelly beans or sugar nonpareils and/or decorating frosting
Marshmallows
Strawberries
Wooden or metal skewers

1. Heat oven to 350°F. Spray small muffin cups (1¾ inches in diameter) with vegetable cooking spray.

2. Stir together sugar, flour, cocoa, baking powder, baking soda and salt in medium bowl. Add egg, milk, oil and vanilla; beat on medium speed of mixer 2 minutes. Stir in boiling water (batter will be thin). Fill muffin cups about ⅔ full with batter.

3. Bake 10 minutes or until wooden pick inserted in center comes out clean. Cool slightly; remove from pans to wire racks. Cool completely. Frost with LICKETY-SPLIT COCOA FROSTING. Garnish with jelly beans, nonpareils and/or frosting piped onto cupcake. Alternate cupcakes, marshmallows and strawberries on skewers.

Makes about 4 dozen cupcakes

Lickety-Split Cocoa Frosting: Beat 3 tablespoons softened butter or margarine in small bowl until creamy. Add 1¼ cups powdered sugar, ¼ cup HERSHEY₃S Cocoa, 2 to 3 tablespoons milk and ½ teaspoon vanilla extract until smooth and of desired consistency. Makes about 1 cup frosting.

Note: Number of kabobs will be determined by length of skewer used and number of cupcakes, marshmallows and strawberries placed on each skewer.

Ice Cream Cone Cupcakes

24 flat-bottomed ice cream cones
1 package (about 18 ounces) white cake mix, plus ingredients to prepare mix
2 tablespoons nonpareils
Prepared vanilla and chocolate frostings
Additional nonpareils and decors

1. Preheat oven to 350°F. Stand ice cream cones in 13×9-inch baking pan or 24 standard (2½-inch) muffin cups.

2. Prepare cake mix according to package directions; stir in 2 tablespoons nonpareils. Spoon batter evenly into cones.

3. Bake 20 minutes or until toothpick inserted into centers comes out clean. Remove to wire racks; cool completely.

4. Frost and decorate as desired.

Makes 24 cupcakes

Note: These cupcakes are best served the day they are made.

Upside-Down Peach Corn Bread Cakes

¼ cup (½ stick) butter
½ cup packed light brown sugar
1 fresh peach, thinly sliced
2 packages (8½ ounces each) corn bread mix
2 eggs
½ cup milk
2 tablespoons vegetable oil
1¾ cups diced fresh peaches or frozen diced unsweetened peaches, thawed

1. Preheat oven to 400°F. Spray 8 standard (2½-inch) muffin cups or ramekins with nonstick cooking spray.

2. Place ½ tablespoon butter and 1 tablespoon brown sugar in bottom of each muffin cup. Divide peach slices evenly among muffin cups.

3. Stir corn bread mix, eggs, milk and oil in large bowl until well blended. Stir in diced peaches. Spoon evenly into prepared muffin cups.

4. Bake 20 minutes or until golden and toothpick inserted into centers comes out clean. Cool in pan 5 minutes. Run knife around edges; invert cakes onto serving plates. Serve warm.   *Makes 8 servings*

Serving Suggestion: Serve with a scoop of vanilla ice cream or whipped cream.

Double-Berry Shortcakes

Filling
- 2 cups fresh sliced strawberries
- 1 to 1½ tablespoons sugar

Sauce
- 1 package (10 ounces) frozen unsweetened raspberries, thawed
- 1 tablespoon sugar

Cupcakes
- 1 package (9 ounces) yellow cake mix *without* pudding in the mix
- ½ cup cold water
- 1 egg
- 2 teaspoons grated lemon peel

Whipped Cream
- ½ cup whipping cream
- 1 tablespoon sugar

1. Combine strawberries and 1 tablespoon sugar in medium bowl. Let stand 30 minutes to 2 hours or until sugar is dissolved, stirring occasionally. Set aside.

2. Place raspberries in fine-mesh sieve over medium bowl. Press raspberries though sieve with rubber spatula. Discard seeds and solids. Add 1 tablespoon sugar; stir until sugar is dissolved. Set aside.

3. Preheat oven to 325°F. Spray 8 standard (2½-inch) muffin cups with nonstick cooking spray.

4. Beat cake mix, water and egg in large bowl with electric mixer at low speed 30 seconds or until moistened. Beat at medium speed 2 minutes. Stir in lemon peel. Spoon evenly into prepared muffin cups.

5. Bake 20 to 25 minutes or until toothpick inserted into centers comes out clean. Cool in pan 5 minutes. Remove to wire rack; cool completely.

6. Beat cream and 1 tablespoon sugar in medium bowl with electric mixer at high speed until soft peaks form.

7. Working with one at a time, split cupcake in half horizontally. Spoon about ¼ cup strawberry filling on bottom half; drizzle with about 1 tablespoon raspberry sauce. Top with 2 tablespoons whipped cream. Cover with cupcake top. Top with 1 tablespoon whipped cream; drizzle with about 1 tablespoon raspberry sauce. Serve immediately.

Makes 8 servings

Tip: To ensure even baking, fill empty muffin cups with 1 tablespoon water before placing in oven.

Acknowledgments

The publisher would like to thank the companies listed below for the use of their recipes and photographs in this publication.

ACH Food Companies, Inc.

Campbell Soup Company

The Coca-Cola® Company

Dole Food Company, Inc.

Duncan Hines® and Moist Deluxe® are registered trademarks of

Pinnacle Foods Corp.

The Hershey Company

Nestlé USA

The Quaker® Oatmeal Kitchens

Unilever

Metric Conversion Chart

VOLUME MEASUREMENTS (dry)

1/8 teaspoon = 0.5 mL
1/4 teaspoon = 1 mL
1/2 teaspoon = 2 mL
3/4 teaspoon = 4 mL
1 teaspoon = 5 mL
1 tablespoon = 15 mL
2 tablespoons = 30 mL
1/4 cup = 60 mL
1/3 cup = 75 mL
1/2 cup = 125 mL
2/3 cup = 150 mL
3/4 cup = 175 mL
1 cup = 250 mL
2 cups = 1 pint = 500 mL
3 cups = 750 mL
4 cups = 1 quart = 1 L

VOLUME MEASUREMENTS (fluid)

1 fluid ounce (2 tablespoons) = 30 mL
4 fluid ounces (1/2 cup) = 125 mL
8 fluid ounces (1 cup) = 250 mL
12 fluid ounces (1 1/2 cups) = 375 mL
16 fluid ounces (2 cups) = 500 mL

WEIGHTS (mass)

1/2 ounce = 15 g
1 ounce = 30 g
3 ounces = 90 g
4 ounces = 120 g
8 ounces = 225 g
10 ounces = 285 g
12 ounces = 360 g
16 ounces = 1 pound = 450 g

DIMENSIONS

1/16 inch = 2 mm
1/8 inch = 3 mm
1/4 inch = 6 mm
1/2 inch = 1.5 cm
3/4 inch = 2 cm
1 inch = 2.5 cm

OVEN TEMPERATURES

250°F = 120°C
275°F = 140°C
300°F = 150°C
325°F = 160°C
350°F = 180°C
375°F = 190°C
400°F = 200°C
425°F = 220°C
450°F = 230°C

BAKING PAN SIZES

Utensil	Size in Inches/Quarts	Metric Volume	Size in Centimeters
Baking or Cake Pan (square or rectangular)	8×8×2	2 L	20×20×5
	9×9×2	2.5 L	23×23×5
	12×8×2	3 L	30×20×5
	13×9×2	3.5 L	33×23×5
Loaf Pan	8×4×3	1.5 L	20×10×7
	9×5×3	2 L	23×13×7
Round Layer Cake Pan	8×1½	1.2 L	20×4
	9×1½	1.5 L	23×4
Pie Plate	8×1¼	750 mL	20×3
	9×1¼	1 L	23×3
Baking Dish or Casserole	1 quart	1 L	—
	1½ quart	1.5 L	—
	2 quart	2 L	—